A GOLF LESSON AT MACHRIHANISH

By J.L. Gubler

A special thanks to Sarah for setting up a blog for this work and to Professor Darrell Spencer for his encouragement to write a book.

CONTENTS

1 A MAGICAL LINKSLAND

I like to play golf. Actually, that is probably an understatement. I *really* like it, but not just any golf. It seems to be a better game when I'm walking down a fairway with a golf bag on my back. I enjoy the time between shots. It is entirely different from riding in an electric cart. In a cart, as irons clank and your golf partner talks, you get to your ball far too quickly. Bouncing around is unsettling and counter to the feeling I want when golfing. It is much more difficult to keep your mind on the task at hand. For me, walking is an important part of the game. Then, if the golf course is something special, that's an added bonus. As luck would have it, I have found that bonus in the form of Scotland's Machrihanish Golf Club.

I first learned about Machrihanish in Michael Bamberger's book To The Linksland. Bamberger starts off describing caddying for Peter Teravainen on the European tour. Teravainen, a Yale graduate called "Whiplash" because of the mach speed of his swing, is a story unto himself. He is a flamboyant, fascinating character to read about. Bamberger then discusses being taught the golf swing by John Stark at Crieff Golf Club. Stark's swing instruction took Bamberger to Auchnafree--to the beginnings of the game. And finally, Bamberger heads to Machrihanish where he describes in detail the beauty of the 1876, Old Tom Morris-designed golf course, Machrihanish Golf Club. He says if he had only one course to play, it would be this one.

I finally got a chance to play Machrihanish at the end of a golf trip with some friends. I said goodbye to them at the Glasgow Airport and then picked up Lydia, my wife, and headed down the Kintyre Peninsula to Machrihanish Golf Club. It is a three-hour drive on a two-lane road. We got there at 9:00 P.M. Still light enough for a quick knockaround, I grabbed my clubs and a couple of Lydia's and headed to the pro shop. Seeing it closed, we went to the tee. We looked out across water and beach to the fairway in the distance. With a peg in the ground and then a swing, there we were, just Lydia and me, walking down the best first hole in golf on a windless summer's evening.

Immediately I saw what Bamberger had written about. Walking off the first tee and heading down the hill, there was a bounce to the turf. The white sand beach on the left stretches four and a half miles from Machrihanish to Westport. The opening shot has to carry from two hundred to two hundred and forty yards of the beach. If you take the shorter carry, the hole becomes a par five. Looking west, the sun lights up the humps of the island of Jura. The Hebridean Sea shimmers like a lake, as the waves caress the beach. This is a nice place.

As we walked along, oystercatchers were feeding in the tide pools on the sand. They lifted off in unison and chirped about our interrupting their feeding. By the time I got to my ball, I was thinking more about the sheer beauty of the place than about my next shot. I can't remember the shots in that round, which is rare for me, but I can remember the evening. The smell of the ocean air and the feel of the moisture on my cheek was a far cry from the desert we are used to. The sand dunes on the course were bigger than Turnberry's and wilder. A ball hit off the fairway and into the grass-covered dunes seemed to disappear underground. Rough does not describe the long whispy grasses that engulf it. You only see one hole at a time. Everything else in view is wild and natural.

After that introduction to Machrihanish, I returned two years later with my golf buddies, George Blues, Chuck L'Hotel, and Doc. By the time we arrived from Loch Lomond that day, Doc was carsick. Even though he had the front passenger seat and the driver went at a medium speed, his face looked white. Although a very picturesque drive, it is a two-lane track, which is a real challenge even for the best traveler. You can avoid the drive by flying from Glasgow to Campbeltown Airport. It probably is a good idea. A guest once asked me, as he staggered out of his car in the

Machrihanish parking lot, if I could have found anything more remote.

Once on the tee, the day was made even better by the fact that my caddie, Ivor Mack, was a member of the club. With only a few holes played, I remembered how much I liked this place. "Ivor, how do I join this club?" "Ay'll git yuuu en epplication whin wi finish." As the golfers had a drink in the clubhouse bar, I quickly filled out the application. Ivor said he would submit it to the membership committee.

Some two years later I received greetings from the club that I had been invited to join. For the nominal sum of two hundred and forty pounds, I accepted the invitation. A few years later I was playing at Glasgow Gailes when a golfer noticed my Machrihanish hat.

"Duuu yuuuu playyy thirrr?" he asked.

"Yes, that's my home club."

"Thettt es thi millionaires golfff courssse," he said. "Therrrr es no whirr en Scotland yuuu can playyy e courssse like thettt end be thee onlyyy golfffer."

He was right. This course is a hidden gem.

MORNING AT MACHRIHANISH

With a cool breeze on my cheek
And squalls on the sea
A braw morning it is at Machrihanish.

And as I look to the West
It catches my eye
On the horizon, a dark spot indeed.
With a rainbow from Eire to Gigha,
It seems to say I'm coming your way.

With waterproofs now on
It starts with a smirr and then something more.
Lasting only minutes it is wet enough.

And then the sun breaks through and backlights the dunes.
They shimmer in the distance as the grasses move.
The wind is now stronger
And off in the distance the sky darkens again.
It could be a dwam, but I hope it's for real.

With a cool breeze on my cheek
And squalls on the sea
A braw morning it is at Machrihanish.

2 KATE

I was pretty excited to get back to Machrihanish as a member. It was a nice feeling having a Machrihanish member bag tag on my golf bag and my fixture list in my pocket. The fixture list is a "wee" book compiled by the Secretary for the members. It outlines in detail competitions for the year and tee times. "Competitions" are member tournaments, which are usually played on weekends. During those competitions the tee is reserved. If you aren't playing in the competition, you aren't playing at Machrihanish.

When I became a member, I made the decision to not play in the competitions. The locals look at the non-resident members a little differently. While they are very nice to the Americans and Europeans, they don't want you winning "their" tournaments. If I played, it would be a no-win situation. I would definitely like the competing. But if I did well in the competition, the locals would look at me as a sandbagger. I wanted to avoid that. I thought it better to blend in.

The other section of the fixture list, describing member tee times, was of more interest to me. Member only times are before 9:00 A.M. Visitors can tee off from nine to noon. Member times begin again at noon. Visitors have another window of opportunity between 2:00 P.M. and 4:00 P.M. The beauty of all this is the members are playing in front of the visitors and thereby avoiding slow play. Even better, if I tee off at 7:30 A.M., I don't see another golfer until I'm coming back in on the 14th. There in the distance I sometimes see a foursome of visitors with caddies plodding along. The speed of play is very important to me. The game is a lot more fun when you can hit it and then go. Having to wait on every shot is not for me. Machrihanish's member times eliminates the waiting altogether.

Another nice thing about golf is if you don't have someone to play with you can still play. Unlike tennis and team sports, you don't have to have a "game." For my first rounds as a member at Machrihanish, I didn't know many people to play with. No matter. As a single, I had the luxury of playing alone. I'm not sure those aren't some of my favorite times. It then becomes the golfer and the golf course. As you walk along to the next shot, the quiet is enjoyable. Likewise, if your ball is going straight, the walk is a shorter distance. It is a nice change not looking for the other player's ball in the tall grasses. That becomes a distraction. As you help in the search for the missing ball, you can hardly wait for it to end, so you can continue with your own game.

The first morning I played as a member, I checked in at the pro shop. "Thi teeeee es yirs," said Hector McDonald, the head pro. No waiting here. A thought flashed through my mind: "I think I am going to like this place."

The first swing at Machrihanish is rather daunting. With the pro shop next to the tee, there is always an audience. As I looked across the beach to the fairway, I tried to choose a line. With the fairway going away on an angle, the more of the beach you take off the shorter the shot to the green. If you don't clear the beach, the ball is still in play. A shot from the sandy beach still leaves a long way to the green. You could take a more conservative approach and aim to the right, but then you bring into play three pot bunkers that you can barely see. They are like magnets. Although small in size, with them side by side, they catch a lot of balls. Once in them, it is a sand wedge out.

Not wanting to let the audience in the pro shop down, I hoped for the best and gave it a go. The golf gods were with me because the ball was well hit and found the fairway. I'm sure the staff in the pro shop breathed a sigh of relief; the new member can play the game. The funny part of that round is that except for my tee shots, I hit three inches behind the ball on every shot for the rest of the round. Perhaps I was suffering from jet lag, or perhaps it was my normal swing fault of sliding.

The boys in the pro shop didn't tell me there was a single in front of me. They probably had a good laugh wondering if I would catch up with him. The reason for the laugh, I would later learn, is that Bobby Blair, the single, is a very interesting character. A retired English teacher, he likes to talk. He is a former scratch golfer who played in several British and Scottish Amateurs. He has the unique accomplishment of winning club championships at five different clubs. Bobby is also an expert, or so he thinks, on many subjects. As I finished the second hole, I saw a player on the third tee. He waved me over. As I walked to him, I thought he was going to let me play through. That would've been nice. "Wuuud yuuuu lik te joinn me?" he asked. My response of yes surprised me. "Thesss es my frinnnd Kate," he said. Kate looked more like a California girl than a Glasgow girl. She was probably the reason I said yes. With straight blond hair to her waist and her sweater and jeans perhaps a little too tight, she made for a good caddy. I was now playing with Bobby Blair.

As we walked to our second shots, Bobby, in a very quick fashion filled me in on his girlfriend, the status of his golf game, his connection with the head pro Hector McDonald, and the price of rice in China. He talked about a lot of different subjects. He also threw in a joke now and then. Unfortunately, I really couldn't understand the guy. Even when he slowed down his speech, it is somewhat of a jumble of words. I tried to nod my head at the right time or laugh when he started laughing. But I had no idea what he was saying.

On my second shot on the 3rd, I had one hundred yards to the green. It wasn't a difficult shot with a wedge, even with the two pot bunkers forty yards short of the green. I proceeded to chunk the ball into the pot bunker. Now I had no shot. At this point, Bobby was probably wondering why he asked me to join him. His caddy knew nothing about golf, so she didn't mind. She probably thought I was supposed to be in the bunker.

Even with Bobby's examination of my swing I continued to hit behind the ball the rest of the round. Bobby shook his head and says, "Thiii svinggg luuuks gooott." The reality, as I look back, was the swaying in my swing. Although the swing looked good, there was far too much movement. Unfortunately, I'd swayed since I was eight. With timing I normally could adjust and hit the ball. However, the game is too difficult to do that on a regular basis. With little sleep on the plane this wasn't going well. I would enjoy the company anyway.

On number twelve, I saw one of the best shots I've ever seen in golf. The hole is a par 5 with deep, large bunkers in front of a raised green. The only time I've seen anyone hit that green was on that day. Bobby said he was going for the green. Even with it down wind I gave him no chance. The ball took off high like an eight iron and, helped by the wind, landed on the green. "Bobby, that's the best shot I've ever seen," I said.

"It wesss gooot," he replied. I could not believe what I had just witnessed. Unfortunately, Kate didn't appreciate it. For her it was just another shot. And for Bobby, as I would later learn, Kate would be just another girl. As time has gone by, Bobby has gone through girls like I go through golf balls.

Meeting up with Bobby on that day was a stroke of luck. This guy is a character. Somewhere between a raconteur and a bon vivant, he is quite full of himself. Additionally, he is a really good golfer. It is interesting how golfers revere better players. Any human failings the scratch golfer has are forgotten. Instead, everyone wants to play with him. His game is something they want, too. They probably won't become that good. However, they'll keep trying to improve to be like him. In the meantime, they are in awe of the way he gets around the golf course. They put up with his failings because he can play the game. Bobby is going to add to the enjoyment of playing Machrihanish.

3 IVOR SARK

It didn't take long to hear from Bobby Blair again. He called me on my cell phone. He didn't realize that the call was routed through the U.S. Bobby was surprised when he got the phone bill. He told me to get a landline.

"Jimmmmm, ettt ess Bobby," he says. "I'mmmm cemmming te Mechrihenishhh nixt weekkk weth enotherr mimber fremm Crieff. Cannn yuuuu pleyyy golff en Tessday end Windsday?"

"That I can, Bobby," I reply.

"Yuuuuu willl likkkk Renalddd McFairrrr. He es a griiit guyy. Wethhh eny luckk we'lll be a furrrsome. I heven't hirrd beck frem thi furrrrth."

"I'll be in the clubhouse around lunchtime awaiting your arrival."

I get to the club at noon the next day. I order a Coke and tell Glynis, the bartender, "I'm waiting for some members to arrive from Crieff."

"Ohhhh," she replies, with a wide grin on her face, "thettt mesttt be Bobbbby endd Runalddd. Theee only cumm whin thi witherrr es goot. Yuuu'll likkke thimmm. Ohhh Runalddd niverr stopps moovingg. He es sooo escittted whin he gitts herre he's like a jittter begggg. Es Ivor cuminggg?"

"I don't know," I reply.

Glynis is from Drumlemble. The name sounds like it comes from Gulliver's Travels. Actually, the little village looks like that. It was built as a company town. The locals were coal miners. The houses are stone cottages approximately six hundred feet in dimension. One hundred people live there. As you leave town headed to Machrihanish, there is another road sign for West Drumlemble. I laugh every time I see it. Where is the town? Glynis is a breath of fresh air. She's the perfect bartender.

This is a wonderful clubhouse. Once a stone mansion, it is a hundred yards from the original clubhouse. At some point the front was added on to provide an open area with large glass windows looking out at the 1st tee and the Irish Sea. In the interest of modernization, the beautiful sandstone was covered with plaster and painted white. Perhaps they wanted it to match the

Victorian Hotel, the Ugadale, next door. In any event it was a mistake. As you drive into Machrihanish, on the left is a row of Victorian sandstone houses and then the clubhouse, which is now white. It sticks out like a sore thumb.

The entrance is a narrow hallway on the side of the building. On the floor is a blue carpet with the club logo, the oystercatcher, used as a background. Immediately over the door the words of Old Tom Morris are displayed, "The Almichity had gowff in his e'e when he made this place." An assortment of old trophies and wooden clubs are in cases. A beautiful wooden plaque painted by hand memorializes each year's club champion. A rogue's gallery of former captains lines the walls. It makes for a comfortable place to sit and talk about the round just played while enjoying a drink.

"Glynis, I think I'll have soup," I say, as I walk toward the cauldron of soup sitting on a table. I was happy to see it was chicken and rice. As I ladle out the steaming soup, I think of how scalding hot food and drinks are served in Scotland. You always have to be careful not to burn your tongue. There is nothing worse than the tip of your tongue singed, as you try to enjoy the rest of the meal. I don't think those taste buds ever come back.

Sitting down at a table next to the windows overlooking the 1st tee, I start thinking about the match to come. My reverie doesn't last long because a bright blue MGA sports car catches my eye. Although of 1960 vintage, it looks like it just came off the showroom floor. I can see that the seats are blue leather with white trim. And then a small baldheaded man with a mustache gets out of the car. He fits the car perfectly. With a well-worn wool sweater that is stretched out of shape and wide rib cords, which are equally worn, he is the man for that car.

As I continue with my soup, I hear a voice behind me say, "Excuse me. Are you Jim Wedge?"

"Yes," I reply. I am now speaking with the man with the MGA automobile.

"I am Ivor Sark. Bobby Blair gave me a call to fill out the foursome."

"Wonderful, we've got a good day for it." After Ivor orders his lunch, he sits down. An old batch of sixty-eight, Ivor is retired from Chiquita Banana's French West Indies location. Originally, from the Shetlands, he speaks as though he is English. That is somewhat odd because many of the people on the Shetlands speak Gaelic. Perhaps with his working so many years out of the country his speech became more proper. The locals call it "proper" English when you can understand what is being said. I learned later that when Gaelic students were taught English in school it was a formal English. That explains Ivor's pronunciation.

On that day he had taken two ferries to get to Machrihanish. The golf course is at the bottom of a peninsula. Living close to Helensburgh, instead of driving down the A83, he took the Butte ferry and then the Porte a Vartie ferry to Tarbert. Apparently, it saves some driving time. Additionally, the ferry rides give you a great view of the water and the land. I later learn Ivor likes to "sail."

"Ivor, I love your car."

"It is a '62 MGA that I've had since it was new," he replies.

"The color is perfect," I say, referring to the bright blue.

"I quite like it. I keep it garaged and it has held up well. There is no rust." That is important to a car guy.

"What else do you drive?" I ask.

"I have a hand-made Gordon Keeble with a Corvette engine that I bought from Lord Harlech. He had it shipped to the U.S. when he was dating Jackie Onassis. When she picked Aristotle Onassis to marry, he had it shipped back. For getting around, I have an MG saloon car." Ivor has a nice stable of cars.

Our conversation then moves on to golf. Looking at Ivor, small in stature with little muscle and a rather professorial look, the uninitiated would think he is a hacker. Guess again. Ivor is a former member of the all U.K. Boys' Team. That is where he first met Bobby Blair. Having played in a number of national amateurs, he was a scratch golfer as a young man. Now at 68, he is a 10 because he has lost some distance off the tee.

That is part of the beauty of the game. You never know by looking at a golfer how he is going to play. If he is dressed in brand-new golf attire, he probably can't play the game. If he talks about how many low scores he has shot, he probably can't play to his handicap. On the other hand, beware of the golfer who doesn't say much about his game. He'll be hard to beat.

Even a good swing can be a misleading indication of how good the player is. The good swing only gets the ball headed in the right direction. From there, all the vagaries of the game seem to pop up: a chunked chip, a skulled bunker shot, a twitch on the backstroke on a three-foot putt. It is amazing how the ball can defy gravity, as it lips out. Until you see the person actually get the ball into the hole, it is hard to guess at how they play.

In Ivor's case his previous accomplishments pretty well tell the story. He can play the game. His swing is almost lyrical. The tempo never changes. The backswing is short, because of the links conditions he has played in. It doesn't look like it generates enough speed. However, the way he keeps the angles and turns his shoulders, there is more force than the eye can see. He still has plenty of distance to play the game.

With him being scratch at one time, you can bet his current handicap is correct. He won't be a "proud" 10. He'll be able to play to his 10, because he knows that is what makes the handicap system work. If handicaps are correct, Saturday matches are a lot of fun. If you can't play to your handicap, the match isn't competitive. Likewise, Ivor would never have an inflated handicap. He respects the game too much. I'm looking forward to playing with him.

4 RONALD MCFAIR

It is not long before Bobby pulls into the car park. The quiet in the room is quickly replaced by a beller from Bobby. "Et'ssss thi Amerrrricen, Jimmmmm Widggggg." Now how do you respond to that? I could only give him a nod of the head and a smile. "Thessss esss Runelddd MaccccFerrr."

"Ronald, it is very nice to meet you," I reply.

"Jimmm," Ronald says in a very clear soft-spoken manner. "Likkwesss. E'vee hurddd e lottt abuttt yuuu." He probably heard about my chunked shots during my last round with Bobby and Kate. I'm sure Bobby enjoyed telling him how the "poor American" was hopeless at hitting the ball. Hopefully things have improved.

Once they get their drinks ordered at the bar, and with them now sitting at the table, the conversation continues. Bobby is quite talkative about his golf game. "I'mmmmm pirttty closss Jimmmmm," he explains. He goes into some detail on the changes the Machrihanish professional, Hector McDonald, is making on his swing. "Enstiddd ef chisssing efterr et likkk thess, I'mmm goinnng te commme ep," he goes on. Ivor gives Bobby a deadpan look during this explanation, as in, "Is this ever going to end?" Apparently it isn't. Bobby stands up and gives us a demonstration of his new swing. "Hirrr et es," he says, as he makes a golf swing back and forth. It will be interesting to see if he can get this swing to the golf course.

It turns out Ivor and Bobby have no love lost on the golf course. They have obviously played too much golf together. First, it was on a national level in amateur tournaments. Even now playing a "friendly" game at Machrihanish, it is obvious they want to beat each other. Every now and then Ivor throws in a subtle remark Bobby's way. More often, though, there is no comment at all on Bobby's good shots. That seems to bother Bobby even more. Apparently, Bobby needs "pats on the back" while playing.

It perplexes me that this would get to Bobby. I never thought a foursome's play should be a mutual admiration society with the players commenting on each other's good shots. The game is hard enough when you are focused on your own game. If I'm spending time looking at the other guy's shot, I'm not spending enough on my own game. I'm surprised that Ivor can annoy Bobby so easily.

But it really affects Bobby's game.

Ironically, Bobby is the last one who should complain. There is nothing worse than your opponent making a critique of every shot you make. "Ohhh, noooo, net thirr," he will say. Or, "Yuuuu wintttt ritttt ovirrr thii toppp ef thitt." Or just, "Thittt wess awfelll." Perhaps it is gamesmanship; I don't know. With Bobby making comments like that, he has no room to grumble about Ivor's subtle humor. Ivor's comments make a person laugh.

5 THE MATCH

With lunch finished we head to the first tee. It is 1:45 and the tee is open. Although a number of visiting golfers are waiting to tee off, the tee is reserved for members until 2:00 P.M. In front of us is a wide-open course. At the tee Bobby asks, "End whett es thee Americenn posssing es firr e hendicapp?"

I quickly respond, "I'm a nine." With Bobby at a 6 we play off his ball. I get three shots, Ivor gets four shots, and Ronald gets eight shots.

"Et es Runaldd end I eqainst yuu twuu en e bistbuull." I wasn't surprised at the teams. I am quite happy to have Bobby on the other team. He is the best player of the group. I figure you will improve if you play against better players. We'll see how this goes.

The first tee at Machrihanish is always a challenge. Practice swings are frowned upon. Usually it is the first swing of the day. The carry over the beach to the fairway requires a well-hit shot. Even at that, if you take the wrong line, the ball will find the beach. If you bail out to the right you can't get home in two. As luck would have it, we all hit good drives and the game is on.

Bobby and Ronald continue commenting on Bobby's shots after he hits the ball.

"Ronald, I cin't hitt itt eny bittter."

"Aye, Bobby, e smesher."

"It feels sooo goot, Ronald."

"Aye, Bobby."

The match is "all square" after four holes. Number 5, Punchbowl, is appropriately named. Looking from the tee to the fairway it looks like a series of craters. The green is not in view. Instead it is over a hill and to the left. Bobby proceeds to hit a snap hook off the tee. "Where dit ettt gooo?" Bobby shouts.

"En thi linnne of thi blu markkkkkerrr," Ronald comes back. "Yerrr en thii longgg gresss," Ronald goes on.

We are playing the medal tees, which makes the hole longer. Perhaps Bobby was pressing to hit it too hard. He has an unusual follow-through, chasing after the ball by staying crouched. As he chases after it, his club flips over violently to the left. It looks like he is always protecting against a hook by staying low to the ground. However, the flipping motion seems to accentuate the hook rather than save the shot.

We walk directly to the spot where Bobby's ball has disappeared in the long grass. It is nowhere to be found. It is buried somewhere underneath where we are walking. Unable to find the ball, Bobby now has a difficult time finding a place to drop. He is still in the long grass with one hundred and sixty yards to the green. The ball settles down in the rough. I don't think he can hit it more than a hundred yards.

Bobby makes the mistake of going for the green. Instead of using a wedge, his seven iron digs into the grass, and the ball moves a foot. Changing to a wedge, he gets back to the fairway, but he now lays four. "Runelddd et es uppp tuuu yuuu," Bobby says. With that said, Ronald proceeds to hit his ball right of the green in an "elephant pit," a very deep depression. From there he takes a five and we go one up.

"Runelddd whet happened," Bobby mutters as they walk to the next tee.

We stay one up through the next three holes. "It's e bonnie dae," cries Ronald as we leave the ninth. Braw and beautiful, this is a great place. Gannets are on the wing in flocks. Large white cumulous clouds dot the sky. The grasses are moving in the breeze, as if they are having a dance. As we walk down the fairway, Ronald sings to me a Celtic song "Westering Home":

Westering home and a song in the air. Light in the eye and it's good-bye to care. Laughter o' love and a welcoming there. Isle of my heart my own land. Ah but it's grand to be waken at day. And find oneself nearer to Islay.

With Islay in view across the Irish Sea, the song has even more meaning.

At the 10th hole, a good par five, Ivor puts a wedge ten feet from the cup on his third shot. "Good job, Ivor," I say. "You can knock that in." Bobby, Ronald and I miss our longer putts. It is now Ivor's turn. With a short backstroke developed from playing windy links golf he rolls his birdie in. "Good job, Ivor," I compliment him again. Ronald has a smile on his face. I ask him what is so funny. "We wuldd nivirrr say goott jobbb," he replies. I better come up with a different expression. I don't want to distract my partner. Thanks to him, we are now two up.

At 12 it is obvious that Bobby is really trying to win. It must come from his competitive days of being a plus 4. One of his biggest claims to fame is a 65 at Carnoustie in the Scottish Amateur, which he has told us about. Obviously, he could really play.

Perhaps that is part of the problem now; he knows how he once played and can't accept how he now does. He tugs his drive to the left, but it is playable. He then proceeds to snap hook a ball out of bounds.

With my feet two feet below the ball, I hit a ball skinny but straight down the fairway. "Thinnn es e robin's coccack," Ronald yells out. I agree. It wasn't pretty, but effective. There aren't many level lies at Machrihanish. Choking up on the club, it isn't easy to hit the ball square. With a wedge onto the green, Ivor and I win another hole. We are now three up.

The game seems to be going our way. The 13th hole has a false front in which the first thirty feet of the green rolls to the front. The only way to get the ball on the green is to roll it on and up that slope or carry your shot over the false front. Ivor decided to go with an eight iron and roll it on. Although it was a bit chunky which helped with over-spin, it ended up pin high at the top of the hill. "Ivor, thet is thi worsse shottt thet evir made thit green," Bobby shouted. Another par and we are now four up.

It is obvious that part of the problem with Bobby's game is that he's always fighting a hook off the tee. On number 14 he does it again. The "mutual admiration society" has become negative. "I jist cin't git thi feeling," he calls out. I can't even watch the swing because it is much too fast. "Thett es sooo bedddd," he goes on.

This match is all but over. On 15 Ivor hits a cut shot with a hybrid within four feet for another birdie. The match ends with us winning five up with three holes to play. As we finish 18, we shake hands and thank them for the game. We also thank them for the two pounds we had each won. "We'll hivve e chinnn wagg en thii clebhousse," Ronald says.

6 LYDIA

I met her in a swimming pool. Actually, I was in the pool reading
The Godfather in 1970 at the house of Don Tripani, the Golden
Gate Hotel comptroller and local banker. He lived through the
block from my parents' house. We didn't have a swimming pool. I
was just back from a semester of college in Hawaii. When I wasn't
selling shoes that summer, I was floating around reading books in
"The Don's" pool.

I knew "The Don" had a niece in town who was working at his
bank. I also knew she had a steady stream of boyfriends visiting
her from Utah. I finally met her one day when she opened the
kitchen door and walked out to the pool.

"Hello, I'm Lydia McGregor," she said. "Can I make you a
sandwich?"

Quite startled by the question I had just been asked by this beautiful girl dressed for work, I said, "No, thank you."

She then asked, "Would you like a glass of lemonade?"

Being the ever romantic, I succinctly replied, "No, thank you."

Lydia, the most beautiful girl I'd ever seen, still smiling said, "Enjoy the pool." Then she turned around and headed back in the house.

When she went in, I thought I would love to take her out, but she wouldn't want to go out with me. My lack of confidence was a result of recently returning from a church mission in England where I had doors closed in my face for two years. Ten hours a day, along with another missionary, we would knock on doors. After two years of that, I returned home somewhat shell-shocked. I couldn't carry on a normal conversation with anyone let alone a pretty girl.

I met her once more that summer. Maxine Spencer invited me to dinner. I thought the invitation was a little odd, since I'd never been invited there before, even though her son Darrell was my good friend. When I went in the house, Lydia was there with Maxine. "Jim, Darrell had to work, and Christine is not home yet. We'll go ahead with dinner without them," Maxine said.

"That's fine," I said.

As soon as dinner was over, Maxine volunteered, "You two should go to a movie." She grabbed the movie section of the newspaper and said, "You'll find a movie in here."

There weren't many movie theaters in Las Vegas in 1970. With one look you could see in the newspaper what was showing. "There isn't anything playing," I said. "Thanks for dinner. I'm headed home."

It wasn't until September at BYU that I saw Lydia again. I was renting an apartment from her parents. I had to go by Lydia's to pick up the key. "Thanks for the key, Lydia. I don't have anything to do tonight. Would you like to go to a movie?" I asked with a sick feeling in my stomach.

"Sure," she said, even though she probably wondered what was the matter with this guy.

With a huge sigh of relief I said, "I'll pick you up at six." I was almost giddy getting in my car and driving to the apartment. I couldn't believe Lydia had said yes.

Picking her up, I opened the door to Lydia's side of the Porsche. I think she was surprised I had a car, since I would always walk over to "The Don's" house to swim. We drove to Salt Lake City to

"The Paprika" on 21st South. We both had steak and lobster in the quiet little restaurant. I can't remember the movie, but when it was over we stopped at a friend's trailer where I had been staying until I got the apartment. The couple was out of town, so I thought we could listen to some music in a quiet place. It was a nice end to a wonderful date.

That was a Friday. By Sunday we decided to get married. However, we didn't let our families know we were even dating during the next four months. I don't think either of us wanted our mothers, along with Don Tripani's wife and Maxine, taking credit for putting us together. During that period those ladies would come to Provo and invite all their children for dinner during their stays. Lydia and I would drive our own cars to the dinner. Other than a hello when we arrived we didn't say another word to each other.

Finally we let our families know. That next summer we were married. Lydia graduated with a BS in computer science from BYU. We moved to Salt Lake City where I went to law school. In retrospect I should have gone to a school in California. Businesses in Utah in 1972 wouldn't hire a female as a computer programmer. Her career in computer science ended before Apple's began.

Although she would have been good at that career, she has been even better at being a wife, mother and now a grandmother. Her sautéed scallops followed with a dessert of vanilla crème brûlèe are to die for. And yes, she looks as good today as she did when she came out of "The Don's" kitchen and asked "Can I make you a sandwich?"

7 HOUSE HUNTING

I like this sixty-five degree weather; it is perfect for golf. Our stays are now quite long at Machrihanish. Each year's stay became longer than the last. One week stretched into two and then even longer. As the holiday expanded, the cost of the trip went up also. Bed & Breakfast houses worked out to seventy pounds a day or twenty-one hundred pounds a month. The price of a rental car for a month was also too much. We ultimately decided it would be cheaper to buy a small house and a reliable car.

We started looking for houses. There were various properties for sale in the area, so we made the necessary arrangements to go and see them. In Scotland, your realtor doesn't go to the showing. Instead, the owner of the property shows the house that he or she is trying to sell. This method encourages "puffing" the property by the owner. As for us, we made sure to say very little about the properties as we looked at them.

The first house, Highspot, was a fairly new build overlooking the park next to the hospital. The owner, who was moving to be closer to his daughter, greeted us. The inside of the house was very Spartan, almost appearing unfinished. Walking in, he pointed out a full bathroom immediately off the front door. That location seemed a bit peculiar. The other two rooms downstairs were a living room and a kitchen. The living room had no furniture. With off-white walls it was a bit drab. Walking into the kitchen the seller exclaimed "Loook," pointing to empty spaces under the counter, "how a wesher end drryer wuldd fit therr end a freezer therr."

"That would be very nice," I replied. As it was, there were blank spaces under the counter for the appliances. A half-sized refrigerator and small oven were the only appliances in the kitchen. The Formica counter top and linoleum flooring the kitchen, although newly built, belonged to the 50's. With the obligatory "thanks" and "we'll get back to you" as we said "goodbye," we didn't like what we saw.

We then looked at a property on the Carradale Road. Surrounded by dairy farms, the white cottage with black trim and a slate roof had a beautiful view of the Irish Sea. In the distance was Ailsa Craig. A very happy lad met us at the door. "Dun't mind thi mess wi aee gitting riddy to meve donn South," he said. As I entered, a fire was going in the fireplace with a very small person sitting close by. I could quickly tell that the fire was not drafting properly. The room smelled like coal dust. As the female sitting down turned around and smiled, she looked more like Yoda than one of the locals.

"Luuk et thi view frum this rumm," the seller said as he directed us to the next room where a very large maroon jacuzzi filled the space.

"A beautiful view it is," I replied. The kitchen had dirty pots and plates stacked in the sink. With the smell of the coal dust filling our lungs, we told the owner we would pass on looking at the upstairs rooms. With a quick goodbye, we had a good laugh as we drove back to Campbeltown. We also began having doubts about finding a house to buy.

Our next house was on the High Street as we drove into Campbeltown. Turning into the driveway we could see a large sandstone mansion built in the 1800's when distilleries were thriving in this area. Met by a young lady at the front door, the foyer had a wonderful Victorian staircase leading upstairs. She was the great-granddaughter of the first owner. As we walked upstairs she explained how she had grown up in the house. She and her husband now wanted to downsize. As we got to the second floor, the ground became quite uneven and creaked as we walked along.

The front windows had a wonderful view of Davaar Island. Clad in heavy oak wood they were beautiful. The ceilings had intricate cornices and decorative molding of a time gone by. The kitchen was expansive. In its heyday, there would have been plenty of space for the servants to each do their various duties as they prepared the food and the house.

Wallpaper was falling off the walls in some rooms. The bathrooms had original tubs and toilets with a chain pull. With years of use, they were stained beyond repair. If we had been looking for a fixer-upper, this house would work. However, we weren't interested in a construction project. I am sure it would wear us out. It definitely would distract from the golf.

"The house is perfect, if we were willing to fix it up, however we don't want to deal with that," I said to the owner.

"I undestendd," she said.

The next house was on a single-track road toward the Mull of Kintyre. We had seen this house numerous times when we had gone out to the Mull. Parking in the driveway we were met with the most beautiful view of Ireland in the distance, as we looked out to sea. The water shimmered in the sunlight. The little cottage sits on a hill overlooking a nine-acre property that rolls to the sea. Streams act as boundaries on each side. Unfortunately, the house is probably too far from the golf course and definitely too far from town for Lydia. The owner welcomed us in. Built in the early 1800's it was sized for the time. The rooms were small and cozy. The owner was doing an admirable job in his presentation, until I asked about the water source.

"Et cumms frim e will. Wii only gitt brownn weter in the summer. En thi shower thi weter es brownn es et goes down thi drain. Et es noooo prublemmm." The brown water ended our interest in the property. As we bounced along the single-track road at twenty miles an hour, it reconfirmed our decision. We were getting nowhere.

"Lydia," I said. "We know of one turn-key property, Ivybank Cottage. Let's go see the Togneri's and ask them if they are interested in selling." Ivybank Cottage is a Victorian House. Built out of stone it had been gutted a few years ago and is a new build inside including plumbing and electricity. Although I had never been inside, Lydia had and liked it. We drove directly to Ivybank while I was feeling brave enough to perhaps make a fool of myself.

Knocking on the door, Helen and Ronald Togneri welcomed us in. They live in half of a beautiful Victorian house that has a separate little cottage with a common wall. Walking into their drawing room, we exchanged pleasantries. Ronald is an artist who is painting landscapes of the area. A product of the Glasgow School of Art, he is doing a good job of preserving this area through his art. After commenting on his new pieces, including a series on Italy where his family is from, I got to the point.

"Ronald," I blurted out, "I had an epiphany last night that you might like to sell the cottage to a nice American couple."

Fortunately, a quick and surprising response came back, "Cumm beck en Thirsday end wi'll heve en enswer fir yuuu." With the somewhat positive reply I thought a quick exit was in order. I was relieved as we left their house. Lydia and I were both happy about the possibility of buying the cottage. I still hadn't seen the cottage, but that didn't matter. Hopefully, on Thursday the Togneris would tell us they are sellers.

To our pleasant surprise when we returned, they said they would sell. I then saw the property for the first time. Walking into the 1820's stone house, which had been plastered on the outside in the 1900's to make it look more modern, I was greeted with wood floors and white walls. The kitchen was obviously from Ikea. It's wood and blue trimmed cabinet doors looked bright. A large window with the original glass in the small panes made the area light up.

In the other direction the living room looked out to a private garden. I noticed the exterior wall was three feet thick where the window was cut out. Double glass doors opened onto the garden. The living room had wonderful furniture with an art deco motif. On the walls hung oil paintings by Mr. Togneri.

Although we didn't know at the time of the purchase, the house came with everything a person would need to move in. Sheets, towels, plates, glasses, broom, vacuum, cleaning supplies, candles. You name it; it was there. One visitor asked if I had a French press so he could make coffee. Telling him I didn't drink coffee, he bought a French press at Tesco. As he savored his coffee at the kitchen table, he looked at the top of the kitchen cabinets. "Jim, you have eight French presses," he said, as he pointed to the cabinets. There in a line was a row of French presses. Yes, the house came complete.

As we stepped into the garden, I was impressed with the ten-foot high stone wall which surrounds it. I am sure from the street view walkers must wonder what is behind that stone wall. The only indication to them of something on the other side is a blue door, which gives access to the street. The garden has a small grass area with a clothesline held up by Victorian poles with finials on the top. A tree shades the area, but there is plenty of room to plant flowers. As you look to the West there are the spires of a Gaelic Church of Scotland a block away. This would be the perfect area to read a book or just sit outside with Lydia.

With the house situation resolved, we went to the Greenbank Garage, a Vauxhall dealer, to find a car. The owner, Roddy McMitchin, seemed like a likable guy. He started us off looking at lower priced cars, which we didn't like. He then directed us to a car he had on consignment, a Vauxhall Meriva. I was a bit hesitant because of the price. "Teke et fir e riide to Caradale. See howw yuu like et." What a clever salesman. Of course we liked it. The car was a turbo diesel with a stiff ride. In the shape of a small SUV, it had plenty of headroom. We bought the Vauxhall.

It is amazing how easy traveling to Scotland has now become. It only requires a briefcase and a passport. No longer do we pack suitcases and bring golf clubs. It's nice not to be tracking down lost baggage. Instead, the clothes and clubs are there at the house. The ownership of a house and a car has extended our summer stay from weeks to months.

8 THE GARDEN

I like the garden behind our house. From the street all you see is a stone wall, ten feet high. A bright blue door is the only indication to the passerby that there is something on the other side. I am sure the occasional walker wonders what is behind that blue door. The door opens up on trash day to take the wheelie bin out for the trash collectors. I've noticed that if someone is walking by while the door is open, they slow down for a good look. To those that catch a glimpse it must seem like someone's "Secret Garden."

The garden is twenty feet by thirty-six feet. The first section, twelve feet deep, consists of a patio with twenty-four-inch square granite slabs. It's a perfect area for a bench, a small shed, and a wheelie bin. From there, a step up brings you to an area composed of gravel and small rocks for a walkway. To the right is a bed of perennials providing a variety of color. Fuschia, roses, a rock garden of alpines, veronica, salix, lupin, penstemon, ligularia, berberis, rhododendrons and begonias fill the area. To the left is a large ash surrounded by a small grassy section. With this being the shady side, ferns, bracken, primrose and a climbing rose occupy the space. At the West end, pyracantha covers the wall. Sweet peas are sprouting up a lattice. A Dawn Redwood stands in the corner. Anemone and gladioli bulbs went in the ground when we arrived. It will be interesting to see how they do planted that late in the season.

Last year, May was cold and June was actually hot. It was a "barbecue" month, so bright and sunny that green vegetation turned to brown including Machrihanish. The course played hard and fast like the locals say it did years ago. It was fun to play it in true links conditions. I wasn't sure the brown grass would ever come back, but it did. This year April was cold but sunny and dry. May was the wettest month since records were kept. June has been great with both sun and rain. Living on a peninsula definitely influences the weather. The Gulf Stream adds to those weather changes making it a micro-climate. From April to September it is hard to guess which month will have the best weather.

Last September, as we were leaving for the states, I hired a gardener from Machrihanish to keep an eye on things. I met her at the Glenbarr Nursery. Saying hello, I asked if she did side jobs. With that question answered I had a gardener. It wasn't until I showed her the garden that I learned she was an organic gardener. I had already mentioned my preference for killing off every slug and snail in the garden, and I now wasn't sure how she was going to handle it. Even if she'd refused to do it my way, I still would have hired her. Although she did an admirable job, the organic gardening did not keep the slugs from getting to the garden before we arrived in May. Apparently, organic gardeners don't mind slugs or the damage they do. The slugs especially enjoyed the dentata ligularia, which has large purple leaves. A beautiful plant, but now with gaping holes in the leaves, it looks a bit sad. I don't think I'll rehire the gardener in the Fall.

As tall as the walls are, it makes for a good combination of sun and shade. It seems quite odd to do little or no watering to maintain it. Usually there is enough rain to keep it wet. A small area of grass sits below the clothesline. It is so small I use hand shears to cut it. Moss competes with the grass. At first I tried to keep it out, but now I like the way it looks.

The garden is a perfect place for sitting outside. It is shaded in the afternoon. With the temperature usually around sixty degrees Fahrenheit the conditions are perfect for reading a book. The town library is well stocked, which is good for me, since I prefer holding a hardbound book as compared to a tablet. Once I finish the *Guardian* newspaper, I open my book. Other than the sound of a few seagulls, it is quiet. The only distraction is some tiny birds, blue tits, which fly from the fence to the "fat balls" and then back. They are entertaining, as they compete for the food.

The garden is unattended for nine months out of the year. It seems hard to believe it can survive with such long absences. It is always a little overgrown when we return. However, cutting back is quite easy. With a little fertilizer as a kick-start, the garden brightens up very quickly with our return. After a couple of weeks it looks quite colorful and well tended. I find it a nice complement to playing golf.

THE CLOTHESLINE

What is it about a clothesline

That is more than a line stretched end to end?

It starts with the poles quite tall in themselves.

Victorian iron with finials on top.

It's really quite grand as it stands there in place

But changes its face when put to use.

As clothes are hung one at a time

It seems as though the line comes alive.

The clothespins are quite colorful, pinned to the line

But then comes the movement that draws your eye back.

A sway of a towel forward and then a snap

A shirt drifting along at a slower speed

And then it's complete with clothes all in place

With everything moving at its own individual pace.

It makes quite a sight, as I stand back and look

No wonder the clothes feel so good when they're dry.

They've just had a dance, the time of their life.

But with the clothes now dry, it comes to an end

As the clothes are removed and the pins gathered up.

With them clean and fresh and now folded away

The line again is just a line.

It will have to wait for another go.

Just give it a day or maybe two

When the clothes hang again the dance will renew.

9 THE PLUMBER

When I get home, Lydia tells me that the plumber came by to fix a plumbing problem. It turns out that after turning on the hot water in the kitchen, she couldn't turn it off. Looking under the sink there was nothing to turn off. The neighbor immediately came over and turned off the main valve in the house, which is located under the kitchen window. With it after 5:00 P.M. he made a quick call to the plumbing company of Wally Nilly. Amazingly, Wally answered the phone. After explaining the problem and that the water was off in the house, Wally said he would be right over. After a quick change of a washer, the water was back on. He said he would be back in the morning to replace the washer on the cold water.

I was off to the golf course before Wally Nilly and his sidekick Tommy arrived the next morning. Lydia and I had decided the night before to have washers replaced in all of the faucets, even though none of them were leaking. Obviously, we didn't want other faucets to fail in the future. That was probably a mistake to plan ahead. With plumbers, never think about avoiding the next mishap. Focus on the immediate problem.

So Wally Nilly and his sidekick Tommy replace washers in all the faucets. When I get home, Lydia informs me that where none of the faucets leaked before, the two in the powder room now leak. Wouldn't you know it? We are heading to lunch, so I quickly jump in the bathtub. After one minute I stand up like I had been shot from a cannon, realizing that the water is scalding me. With perhaps permanent injuries to my rear quarters, I realize there is only hot water. Somehow in replacing the washers, Wally Nilly and his sidekick Tommy have cut-off the flow of cold water to the bathtub.

On the way to lunch I stop into Wally Nilly Plumbing, advertised as doing "new build" as well as repairs. The young receptionist is shocked when she hears we have no water in the tub. With a gentleman standing in the small waiting room, she assures me that although Wally Nilly is not available, someone would be there this afternoon. Turns out Wally Nilly must have been hiding in the back because once Lydia and I sit down at the Bluebell Restaurant for lunch, Lydia says, "There is Wally Nilly," who is now with the same guy I'd seen minutes earlier in Wally's waiting room. This is the first time I have seen Wally Nilly. He does not look as I expected, as the owner of a plumbing company. Instead, his uncombed hair tops off grease-covered Levis and a sweatshirt.

Taking the lead from Lydia I stand up and say, "Wally Nilly, it is nice to meet you."

Before I can get to the plumbing issue Wally Nilly, a Machrihanish member, wants to talk golf. "How's yir golf gime," he asks. "I jist pleyed in the cleb championship end aftir losing my bell on the seventh hele I wilked in, because thi wether wis miserable."

"Hasn't been the best weather," I say.

"Ahc, it is biin offul," he says.

"Wally Nilly we have no water in the tub and the sinks leak."

"I will bi ova riit aftir luunch," he replies.

I wait all afternoon for the plumber to show. He doesn't come. Meanwhile I realize we have no water in the two toilets. With the tanks hidden behind the walls I finally figure out how to remove a counter in the powder room, so I can at least fill up the tank.

Now I am mad. I may never see Wally Nilly again. Fortunately, my neighbor tells me Wally Nilly meets his crew at 8:00 A.M. every morning. With that tip, I am at his shop at 8:00 A.M. I spot him. "Wally, you didn't come by like you said you would."

"Dint iny won cumb by?" he responds.

Remaining calm I say, "No, no one came by and we are without water."

With a horrified look he replies, "Tommy and I er cuminggg rit naw. Waiit, lit mi til ma boyss where ta guu."

"Fine, I will see you at the house," I respond. As I'm walking to the house, I realize I made a cardinal mistake. Never let the plumber out of your sight when you have him in a corner. Luckily, after a couple of anxious moments, Wally Nilly and his sidekick Tommy show up.

The dynamic duo is now on the run. On entering the house they run upstairs to the tub. Turning on the tap there is no cold water. They look at each other in disbelief. I suggest to them it is probably an air lock. Wally Nilly starts pounding on the tap trying to take it apart. He gets it apart and removes the valve, but there is still no water. Again he and Tommy have a long stare at each other in amazement. Wally Nilly now tells Tommy who has been standing watch to go get a ladder out of the truck.

"Thirrr iss e coffiiin tenk in thi ettic. Lit's chick itt," he says.

"Oy," Tommy replies and is off running for the ladder. I now see Tommy with the ladder and Wally Nilly on his heels again running up the stairs, which makes a hundred and eighty degree turn halfway up. They are starting to look like the Keystone Cops. Before I can get up the stairs I hear them running back down the stairs with Tommy in the lead.

"Thi lidderr is ta shott," Wally Nilly yells. "We ir goin ta git anithirr one."

Off goes the truck with Wally Nilly and his sidekick Tommy in it. I hope they come back.

Twenty minutes later they arrive back. Running up the stairs with the longer ladder, with Tommy in the lead, I am amazed they make it around the paintings on the walls. These guys move fast. With the ladder in place, it is still four feet short of the twelve-foot ceiling. No matter. With Wally Nilly holding the ladder Tommy, all 110 pounds of his cigarette-nourished body, scampers up the ladder. Opening the attic door he pulls his sixty-one-year-old frame into the attic like a cat burglar.

"Oy," he says after a minute. "Thi fill on thi cuffinn tink is closed."

Wally Nilly turns to me and says, "Did ya cluse itt?"

"Wally, I don't have a ladder. The last person in the attic was your plumber who installed the new plumbing ten years ago."

"Oy," he responds.

I suggest again it is an airlock. Once Tommy comes back down and after the two of them look at each other for a long period, Wally announces, "Tummy, I think it is en erlock." Now I am a little relieved. The boys are headed in the right direction. "Tummy, wi nied ta bluuu it utt," he says. "Wi willl go git a hossse." Running down the stairs the two are in their van and off again. Thirty minutes later they return with a garden hose. It wasn't quite what I expected. I was expecting a hose with a pressure tank.

Back in the attic goes Tommy with the hose. With Wally Nilly at the tub Tommy starts blowing. "Oy, Tummy it is duinng nuthinn. Keeep blowiiin Tummmy," he adds. Now really, how long can little Tommy, whose lungs have been saturated with nicotine for sixty years (he didn't start smoking until he was one), keep blowing? The odds are he is going to pass out in the coffin tank in the attic. Maybe that is where it gets its name. With the blowing continuing a spurt of water comes into the tub. "Tummy, keeeep blowiin, wi've git waaterr." A little more water comes in. With the blowing continuing, it is obvious Tommy played the trumpet in his younger years.

Wally Nilly is hurriedly putting the valve back in the tub before water goes everywhere. "Tummmy, cummm downn." Tommy reappears. I can now hear in the background the toilet tank filling up in the master. These guys are good.

I then inform them the two taps with the new washers in the powder room are leaking. Tommy proceeds to take the valves out and replace them with new ones. Two days before they had replaced the washers by trimming some over-sized washers to fit the valves. Obviously, that "band aid" fix resulted in them leaking. Wally Nilly watches his sidekick Tommy, as the valves are replaced. The job is done. With that I hurry to meet my buddies from Crieff, Ronald McFair and Bobby Blair, for an afternoon competition.

When I get back from the golf Lydia tells me that the cold-water tap in the powder room leaks. Without saying a word I have already thought out the solution to that problem. I'm going to buy a couple of crescent wrenches and Teflon tape and repair it myself. I am done with Wally Nilly. Well, almost. He told me to walk by his office sometime and pick up the bill. Lydia asks me if the attic door was black before the cat burglar climbed into it. Shaking my head, I head next door for a ladder. With a Mr. Clean sponge, Tommy's greasy handprints disappear from the attic door.

A couple of days later I pick up the bill. Without any itemization, Wally Nilly has arrived at a figure of two hundred and forty pounds, which I am sure includes turning on the inflow to the coffin tank which he hadn't done ten years ago when he installed it, replacing washers which he then replaced with valves a day later, travel time to pick up a longer ladder and subsequently a hose, and Wally Nilly standing around while his sidekick Tommy did most of the work. Normally, when you see a bill like that you would tell the plumber to itemize it. However, in this case, not wanting to appear like the cheap American and not wanting to ever see Wally Nilly and his sidekick Tonto—no, that is Tommy—again, I bite the bullet and pay the bill.

Will I have Wally Nilly in the future? The answer is no. With me standing over the Keystone Cops when they weren't running up and down the stairs, I learned how to replace the valves. I now know where the main water shut off is. Curiously enough, there aren't shut offs for each sink. We are now in good shape to do our own plumbing in the future. Remember! Never ask a plumber to do more than he needs to. And if his name is Wally Nilly, get a different plumber.

10 THE WHEELIE BIN

The weather has changed; it is springtime at Machrihanish. The daylight hours are very long. With that I decide to get up early this morning for a round of golf.

Sliding out of bed at 6:45, I do my best impersonation of a church mouse, so I don't disturb Lydia. I remember to get the wheelie bin out for the garbage men. By 7:30 I am ready to go. With clubs in one hand and shoes and hat in the other, I consider leaving the door unlocked but decide not to. Upon reaching the car I realize I don't have the car keys. Thoughts come quickly to my mind: Did I leave the garden gate open when I took out the wheelie bin? No. Did I leave the front door unlocked? No.

Needing a plan to get back inside, I notice that the neighbor's storm door is open. They are awake. On the opposite wall of the garden we have an adjoining garden door. They will have a key to that, as well as the back. These are wonderful neighbors. I give the front door a knock but no one answers.

Plan B consists of me throwing my dental floss at the second floor window where Lydia is sleeping. At first I thought I would throw a rock. However, I opted for the floss. It seems to accomplish the desired effect. Whack, whack, whack...on the window. But unfortunately, it doesn't wake her up. Without her hearing aids in, she really can't hear.

Plan C. At this point I'm not thinking very clearly after my previous failed attempts. To bring the story to life really requires it to be written with the letters "ie" at the end of the words which mimics how the locals would describe what happened next.

I decide that if I do a climbie on the wheelie binnie, my hands will reach the toppie of the wallie. I can get to the toppie and then droppie downie to the sheddie on the other sidie. Helen, the neighbor, had told me of 13-year-old Jack who was going over fences regularly. If Jack can do it, I can too. In fact our ages end in the same last number. It might not be a coincidence.

With the plannie in placie I put the wheelie binnie next to the stonie wallie. Climbing on to the binnie I am now ready to stand up tallie reaching my hands over the ten-foot high wallie. In a somewhat continuous motion, lasting probably two seconds, as hands touch the toppie, the wheelie binnie starts rolling towards the harbor. I grab onto the wallie tighter feeling mossie on my handsies and gravity brings me abruptly downie. With my weightie still on the binnie I begin to fallie sideways with the wheelies racing out which provides a sliddie for me to droppie to the groundie.

Amazingly, I am still in one piece. A scrape on the palm of my hand and a scrapie to my watch are the only injuries. Thinking more clearly now, after a reprieve from permanent injury, I go back to the Togneris'. Knocking louder this time, the door is answered. After explaining I am locked out, they get the key and let me in the side gate. The back door is open and I go in and get the keys. Without waking Lydia I head to the golf course.

Looking back I've decided I'm going to be more careful around or outside the house. Accidents are just a step away. If I'd broken bones, I wouldn't be playing golf for some time. I am glad I don't have to explain to Hector McDonald why I'm in traction. I can imagine his response, "Yuuuuuu dedddd whetttt?"

11 THE CADDY MASTER

My cottage is around the corner from the Ardshiel Hotel. The hotel's popular whisky bar is a meeting place for some of the locals. I decide to go say hello to Billy, the Caddy Master at Machrihanish. As I start up the walkway to the hotel, I can see the back of Billy in the window of the bar. Billy spends most evenings sitting next to the bar in that position. As I walk in he says, "Jimmmmy yir beck." "Aye," I reply. With a lager in front of him I ask what would he like to drink. "How bout e shot if Springbank whisky?" The Scots love their whisky. For me it's a diet Irn Bru. It looks like ginger ale. With a bitter taste it is just bearable.

"How have you been Billy?"

"Net thit welll. I've hed three strokkkes sinse yuu lest saw me."

"I'm sorry to hear that, Billy."

"Thi lest strokkke I wes releasedd frem thi Glasgow Hospitall en e Saturday end on Monday I went withh Malcolm te St. Andrews. In thi efternoonn we pleyed Kingsbarn. Thi nixt day it was the Dukes course. En Wednesday it was thi New Course at St. Andrews end thin we drovvve beck to Campbeltown."

"Billy, it sounds as though you've had a fast recovery."

"Willll ets my short termmm memory thet isn't thet goottt," Billy says.

"It could be worse," I reply.

I like Billy. Somewhat philosophical at this point in his life, at times in the conversation he stares at the whisky lined up on the bar shelves. His facial expression looks like he is trying to figure out how to squeeze himself into one of those bottles.

Malcolm McSwain and his wife come into the bar looking for the elusive Gene Howard from Connecticut. Gene is a whirling dervish who never knows where he is until he arrives. He doesn't show up at the bar, which is better for me. I am not interested in playing with him during his short stay in Machrihanish. He never stops talking on the course. One of the pleasures of walking on the golf course is the solitude. I try to avoid the chatter there.

"Jimmm, thi greennns were awfel en February. Eighteeeen

timporarrries. Et niverr heppenned bifor," Malcolm says.

"I'm glad I didn't arrive any earlier. They're putting good now," I reply.

"Aye, thirrr ceminggg elllongg."

We talk a little about American golf and the Senior Open at Troon, which Freddie Couples just won. We chuckle about Freddie getting a slow time playing with the slowest player in golf, Bernard Langer. Freddie replied half-cocked that there would be trouble if any other penalty were imposed on the slow play. I wish they had penalized him a shot. I would have enjoyed seeing what "trouble" would come from Freddie.

"Jimmm wi heve en opening en Tuesday wuld ye likkke to play?" Malcolm asks.

"Absolutely."

"Whyyy denn't ye pickkk es ep en frent of thi White Hart Hotel at 8:30 end wi'll ge frem thir," Malcolm replies.

I tell him I'll be there. These boys either take a bus to Machrihanish or have a designated driver, so they can drink after golf. On this occasion I'm the driver.

Tuesday is a beautiful bright morning with the wind coming from the land. After throwing up balls to determine the teams, and establishing the handicaps, we are off. A best ball format, I get Eddie, a 16, and Malcolm gets Billy. Malcolm and I are playing even as 6's. The first hole is dead into the wind. Although a par four, it is a three wood for a second shot. Still eighty yards from the green I hit a wedge "stony." Before I putt, Eddie sinks his for a 4, and we win the hole to go one up. The second hole is still into the wind. The other three cannot clear the mound in front of the green. With a chip from the edge of the green and a one-putt we are now two up.

From the 3rd tee the golfer is looking at the Irish Sea with Islay and Jura in the distance. The Paps of Jura give it a mystical air. Looking down the fairway there is a white and red marker at the top of a hill. That marks the line to take for your drive. The shot is made even more difficult because the wind is blowing left to right. Even professionals find that to be the most difficult wind in golf. The tendency is to double cross and hit the ball left. Malcolm and I find the fairway. He then gets on in two with a fairway wood. I hit an eight iron with the ball going right at the hole. After Malcolm misses his putt, we are three up. Malcolm whacks his ball violently off the green and says, "Et es net mee dayyy."

The short 4th hole proves the point that a par three doesn't have to be long to be good. I've played the one hundred twenty-five yard hole many times when no one in the foursome hits the green. It sits there like a raised tabletop. The green is effective in rejecting balls hit into it. I'm not sure how hard to hit the eight iron. Looking good in the air it ends up in the bunker short of the green. "A Lizzzz Taylor," says Billy. "Beautifullll bet e litttle fattt." I'm glad Billy can still remember his repertoire of jokes.

With a par on 5 we are four up after five. On the 6th tee Malcolm remarks, "Threeee timmmm club chempionnn end wirrr downnn firr efter fivvve." He lets out a laugh. After they win the 8th, Malcolm laughs again. Now only three down he says, "Wi're en er way." A few holes later, as Billy uses a pitching wedge from an awful lie to try to move it down the fairway, although the green is over two hundred yards away, he remarks, "Eh man mist knowww hisss limitations." Good course management is necessary to play here.

Their luck doesn't change on the back nine. It is nice to beat the former club champion three ways. I buy the first round of drinks in the bar. As we sit down, we talk more golf. Eddie talks about an encounter he had with Tim Finchem, the PGA Tour Commissioner. Eddie, at the time the Captain of the club, and his group were teeing off number 1 when a Chinook helicopter landed in the first fairway. When they got to the helicopter, with the air from the blades buffeting them and hats going airborne Eddie asked who was in charge. Finchem came out and Eddie said, "Whet ere ya doinggg lendingg e helicopter en thi fist fairway?"

Finchem replied, "I must have been misinformed."

"Wi'll git thet thing out ef thi fairway end off yeh gooo."

The PGA Tour Commissioner, without saying anything more, sheepishly got back in the helicopter. With the pilot informed of the Machrihanish Captain's displeasure it took off and landed in a suitable area.

After a few more drinks, we head back to town. "I'll be glad to take each of you home," I say. The boys won't hear of that.

"Noooo, jest droopp es et thi White Hart Hotel," Malcolm says. It wasn't until weeks later that I realized they weren't heading home after golf. Instead, they went in the White Hart Hotel for a few more drinks. These fellows are a hearty lot. All three are close to 70. They've just walked eighteen holes. And now they're off to have a few more drinks.

12 INTRODUCTION TO A NEW SWING

The sun wakes me earlier than expected. I didn't close the storm shutters last night because I was enjoying the streetlight flickering through the leaves of the tree outside the window. With the clear sky and the sun out, I'm glad for the early start. Also, today is the first round of the 2011 U.S. Open.

Driving to Machrihanish, my thoughts are on the U.S. Open. Unfortunately, Tiger Woods is out with a leg injury. That is too bad, because a major is not the same without Tiger in the field. All the talk is about Luke Donald, Lee Westwood or Martin Kymer winning. The reality is at least thirty different players could win at Congressional. Playing the longest of any U.S. Open course at approximately 7,560 yards and a par of 71, I give the edge to the longer players.

As I tee off, before the pro shop opens, it is one of those perfect mornings at Machrihanish with no wind and the sun shining. When I can hear the skylarks above me, I know there is no wind, since their high-pitched sound only register with me on a calm day. I damaged my ears shooting shotguns and high-powered rifles when I was growing up. We didn't use earplugs. The sound of the larks adds to the beauty of their hovering with wings frantically moving. They are a wonderful sight. I enjoy hearing them for the whole round. Afterwards, I decide to say hello to the pros in the shop.

After the normal hellos and talk about the weather, our conversation turns to golf instruction. I had previously mentioned to the pro, Hector McDonald that I wanted to take lessons. In his office now he shows me YouTube clips of Louis Oosthuizen, Robert Rock (who won last week), Ben Doyle (the guru at Quail Lodge in Carmel who is a Golfing Machine proponent), and Mac O'Grady. He says Rock credits his recent win to MORAD (Mac O'Grady Research and Development).

I mention that I was looking at Sam Snead's backswing last night. I noticed his back bends to the target at the top of his swing. Hector McDonald then stands up and shows me how to bend. "Whin I wis a boyyy I naturally straightened my rihttt leggg on thi beck swing," he says. "I hit my irons solidly. However, David Leadbetter got me te change te bending thi rihttt leg. Whin Ben Doyle came ovir hirrr te look et Machrie Golf Club fir e pussible purchase, I tuld himmm ebout my quandry. He said, 'Why wouldn't you want to straighten your right leg?' Sooo aye wint beck te my olddd swing, viryy similar to Stack and Tilt, surrre enuffff I hittt thi balll solidly egain." McDonald's back bends to the target like Snead's when the club reaches the top.

I ask who they like for the Open. Both Luke Donald and Lee Westwood come up. I ask them to guess who Bobby and Ronald McFair will be cheering for. In unison they respond correctly: Stephen Gallacher. If Gallacher gets in the Masters, Bobby and Ronald are going to the Masters. I told them not to forget a badge for their American friend. Ronald McFair is a former Captain of Crieff Golf Club and good friends with Bernard Gallacher, a former Ryder Cup Captain, and his nephew Stephen. I hope he makes it to the Masters, so they can go to the tournament. Every golfer needs to see Augusta National at least once.

Hector invites me to come over to watch the Open. I tell him my Sky Sports subscription will be up and running by Friday with any luck. "I may take you up on your offer, if I still don't have Sky. I'll be back at 3:00 P.M. to watch the first round in the clubhouse." In the UK, Sky, a paid subscription, has the majors locked up. Without it, you don't see those tournaments.

I walk across the street to the clubhouse to see the Steward, Iain. I want to buy raffle tickets he is selling for a set of irons, as well as for his upcoming charity event for injured soldiers. Last year I won six bottles of wine in the event. He had previously told me he was too busy to round up prizes like he had last year, so he thought he would just have a raffle board.

"Iain, I will bring back the wine I won, so you can put it in your charity raffle," I offer.

"Thet es viry kind of yuuu."

"Do you have a box I can put it in?" Quickly disappearing and then reappearing he handed me a box for the wine. "I will bring it back this afternoon, when I come to watch the Open."

"Thet willl be fine," he says.

At the house I open the cabinet for the wine to see five unopened bottles. The other one has been opened. Apparently, Lydia used it to cook. I'll pick up an extra bottle at Tesco.

As I drive to town, I decide to place a bet at Scotbet. I put a "tenner" on Dustin Johnson at 25-1 and another "tenner" on Ryan Moore at 60-1. It will add a little interest to watching the tournament. I'm looking forward to this U. S. Open.

13 THE U.S. OPEN

I learn that my subscription to Sky Sports will not start until the weekend, so I accept Hector McDonald's offer to watch the U.S. Open at his house. With the time difference it doesn't come on until 9:00 P.M., but it is worth staying up late to watch the U.S. Open.

Hector McDonald is from Gullane. One of his first golf jobs was as an assistant at Elie, a wonderful Open qualifying course. He has been at Machrihanish some ten plus years. His golf shop next to the first tee is detached from the clubhouse. A stone building with a slate roof, it is quite small but a retailer's dream inside. With shelves on all the walls and the clothing neatly folded, it is a marketing marvel. It has everything, from waterproofs to range balls. What is even better than his merchandising, Hector McDonald knows a lot about the golf swing. It will be fun to watch the Open with him.

With Rory McIlroy running away with the tournament we find ourselves talking about golf as much as watching it. He asks me if I have read any of Stan Utley's books on the short game. When I tell him that I have not, he says, "Yuu know yuu cen buy boooks, Jimmm." He has a very dry sense of humor. I ask him to tell me about how he gets out of a bunker. He leaves the room and comes back with an Utley book. Opening it to the chapter on bunker play, he goes through the pictures. To my surprise Utley doesn't swing outside and cut across the ball, as I have always been told. Instead, he has a tight inside swing and using the bounce of the club hits consistent shots.

Hector says, "I used te hittt them thin et times, bittt nowww I dun't." That has always been my problem with bunker play: some good shots, but plenty of thin ones. Hector then asks, "Jimmm, du yuu hittt your balll low?" And before, I could answer he continues, "I elways hittt thi ball low whin I wes a boy. I cuuld hittt et under e car. Thi firther I kept my weight beck, thi lower it wint." I'm sure he brought the subject up, because he has seen my tee shots off the first hole at Machrihanish. They have a low flight. Hector then grabs a club that had been shortened and starts swinging in the living room. As he swings slowly, he says, "You've git te cummm out of thi grounddd faster. Thet es all et isss." He shows me photos of various golfers from Ben Hogan to Nick Faldo, pointing out each of their positions at the finish. He says that Hogan has "cummm out of thi grounddd." Faldo, in these photos, has not. I'm not sure what he means by that expression. "Yuuu know, whin Faldo fisttt came en thi tourrr he wes veryyy longgg. Wince he wint te Leadbetter his drives, although streittt, only wint two hundred end fefty yards. Loook et thet position. His belt es level. He isn't out of thi grounddd. This es whirrr yuuu need te beee." He finishes his follow-through with his belt up and his back bent. "Yuuu have te cummm out of thi grounddd faster." It is now making more sense to me. I first thought he only meant the club had to come up. However, it is the extension of the back on the downswing that makes the shot come out of the ground.

Hector continues, "Yuuu know how Nicklaus cuuuld hittt thet power fade?" I don't know, but I listen intently. "He wuuuld open his stance end coming frommm thi inside, loook how mich fartherrr thi buttt of thi clubbb es from thi ball than onnn e square stance. He wuuuld thennn cummm out of thi grounddd. Thet es how he cuuuld hittt e two ironnn both farrr end high." I never had any idea how good players could do that. The only fades I had ever seen by the average golfer were weak shots to the right. Nicklaus changed my opinion of a fade. At the Tournament of Champions in Las Vegas in the 60's I was amazed how he was the only player who could reach the par 5 5th hole and do it with a two iron. The ball had the trajectory of an eight iron with a fade that just kept flying.

"Loook et Rory," as he puts the television in slow motion, "he es right ovir thi ball end his head staysss centered thruuu thi swinggg." McIlroy's performance in this Open is like a clinic: three hundred yard plus drives in the fairway with wedges into the greens. "Loook et his puttting." Hector has not stopped the television. "Thi stroke es mech shorter with nooo recoil. Right efter hisss melt down et thi Masters he wint to Dave Stockton end loook how he hes helped him. Stockton nivir wes e goood striker of thi balll, buttt his short game wes phenomenal."

"Heve yuuu seen Utley's puttting device?" he asks. I haven't. Going into the next room he comes back with a board with an arc. "Loook et thisss," as his stroke goes back and forth. He has me try it. Your first thought, since there is an arc on the board, is that the club is opening and closing. However, once Hector puts his club horizontal to the ground and on my shaft pointed on the line, I can see the club stays square. I have always made a lot of putts, but I think my putter head goes outside as I take it back. I have always thought I would pull the ball if it went inside. Now I can see that the club head actually is still square to the target when it is on the arc on Utley's board.

I ask him about where your weight should be on a driver. With my driver, I have to get my weight on the inside of my right foot on the back swing to hit it good. "Nooo," he says. "The weiittt es still on thi lefttt, but because thi clubbb es longer end thi balll forward, yuuu need to push out yourrr lift hip forward."

Our discussion doesn't stop there. We talk about Mac O'Grady, who spent a lot of time in the 1980's at the Desert Inn Country

Club when I was a member. Everyone on the staff at the club was using O'Grady's method. At the time, I found it too confining, so I continued with what I had. O'Grady never explained clearly what happened in the backswing: how exactly the player goes from flexion to extension. Not knowing about extension then, I couldn't figure out how to keep my arms connected to the body. When I would try it and still stay in flexion, I felt like I was all tied up.

Hector is familiar with Mac, because in recent years he has come to Scotland to do clinics with the Scottish pros. Hector says O'Grady always starts out the same way telling how Seve Ballesteros didn't pay him for lessons. Seve owed him some forty thousand dollars according to Mac. Mac had only negative comments about Seve. The truth of the matter probably is that Seve didn't see any results from MORAD. Seve obviously couldn't make the change from his natural free swing to the structure of Mac's teaching. During that time Seve's golf got even worse. I remember seeing him on TV tee off at an Open. His snap hook went one hundred and fifty yards into the grandstand the first two days. Seve probably thought he didn't owe anything, because he got no results.

"Wheyyyy es et thit with guys like Seve and Arrrnie who err 'ladies men' that men like them as much as women?" Hector then answers his own question: "Perhaps men see something in thim that they weesh they haddd...almost like their alter egooo." He nods as he continues thinking. I remember standing close to

Arnold Palmer as he hit balls on the driving range during the Tournament of Champions at the Desert Inn. He kept talking to the spectators. Before the next shot he would hitch up his pants and make another swing. His persona was like electricity. Both the men and women watching were equally captivated. On the other hand it is easy to see why Arnie's Army did not accept Jack Nicklaus, when he first arrived on the tour. Nicklaus was boring. He was overweight and all business. He would pull out his yardage book, a first for the tour. After a great deal of delay, he would then hit a great shot. For the golf fans at that time he was the opposite of Palmer.

We didn't see much of the U.S. Open on those two nights. The conversation went on nonstop. I have forgotten some of the lessons Hector gave me. However, I will never forget the excitement in his voice, as he described the game of golf. Equally exciting for me was what I learned. I regretted that my Sky Sports was working by Saturday. I wanted to keep hearing Hector talk about the game. He made those first two days very special. From what he said I might be able to change my golf swing.

14 THE SCOTTISH LADIES' AMATEUR

In June of 2011, Machrihanish hosted the Scottish Ladies'
Amateur. It is part of their Rota. The players love coming to
Machrihanish. I picked the players up on the back nine and
watched them finish their round. The wind was howling. It is the
type of day where you should find something else to do.
Unfortunately for the girls, they didn't have a choice. I was
impressed with how hard they hit the ball. Their shots bored
through the wind.

The caliber of golf was excellent. I watched Ellie Shrug win two
matches. One of the youngest of the players, she putted like a
youngster, banging them in the hole with no fear. The final the
next day matched Shrugg from Malaig against Belle Bustrom from
Pitlochry. I decided to go back out in the gale force winds. The
golf was too good to miss. I expected Ellie to win, since she never
missed a putt the day before. I hadn't seen Belle play.

Waking up to a howling wind and rain I gave the pro shop a call to see if the start time had been delayed. Craig responded, "Nuuu, thi ledddies err uff." It was probably a silly question. Competitions aren't delayed at Machrihanish for weather. The turf is on sand dunes. Rain goes right through the ground. There is rarely even a puddle.

I decide that I will pick up the match at the 10th green. The big question is what to wear. I opt for Wellingtons and my waterproofs. Fortunately, the jacket has a hood. In difficult conditions you can button it down with only your eyes and nose showing. It is not the most fashionable outfit but functional. I consider an umbrella but change my mind. In this wind, it would turn inside out.

Parking my car at the practice range I cannot believe the conditions. With a smirr and 40 mile per hour gusts, this is not a good day. Actually, I've only played Machrihanish once in weather this bad. When I finished that round, I wondered why I had played. It is painfully difficult like that.

The match has not reached the 10th, so I sit down on a bench below the 11th tee. Others quickly join me, including some girls who had played in the tournament. They have a gift of gab. The night before they enjoyed the pubs in Campbeltown.

"Yuur thi Emericann frumm Las Vegass?"

"Aye," I respond in a Scottish retort.

"Cenn wi vesitt yuuu en Las Vegas?" she goes on. Feeling no pain from the night before, she has her eye on traveling. With my e-mail in hand, Susan Wood, an optometrist from Edinburgh, may show up in Vegas someday.

To my surprise as the players come up the 10th fairway the leader board shows Belle 2 up. They are both short on the par 5. It soon becomes 3 up with a missed putt by Ellie. The wind is howling out of the Southeast making the par 3 11th a driver. Both ladies leave their shots right and short with difficult chip shots left. Ellie misses her putt as the howling wind blows it left on the edge. Belle makes hers. She is 4 up with seven to go.

This is the first I have seen of Belle Bustrom. She is not what I expected. An international player she is quite tall and gangly for a golfer. Looking more like Ichabod Crane, you would expect her on the prêt-à-porter runway. Whereas the other girls are wearing beanies, Belle has on a rakish looking unshaped hat, more like Isadora Duncan. With a wonderful tight swing she is a pleasant sight. I had seen Ellie the day before. She is an athletic looking golfer with an equally good swing, keeping her right elbow tucked into her side with her arms and body staying connected.

Fortunately, there is a good crowd composed mostly of competing players who had been eliminated. Some of them are trying to hold onto umbrellas with little success. Most of them look very wet. I keep my back to the wind to avoid the rain coming sideways. These are really difficult conditions. If the wind were any harder, it would be a gale.

Number 12 is a par 5. The wind is blowing left to right. Ellie's third shot is still 200 yards from the green. She hits a great fourth shot that ends up over the green. Belle is short right in some tall grass. A magical green with the pin in a bowl in the back, Belle gets within six feet. Shrugg, with her ball down a slippery slope on the back, is a similar distance away. Both ladies miss their putts.

The 13th is dead into the wind. It is close to fifty miles an hour. Both ladies put it in the fairway. Ellie then comes up short of the green, and Belle tugs her shot left. Ellie is long with her third, and Belle is still short. Both chips end up ten feet away. Ellie leaves another putt on the lip, which results in another halved hole. As she walks off the green, she is noticeably upset as she comments to her caddy, her dad.

The 14th should be called the Long Hole, because of its shear length. As I walk up the fairway, a gentleman catches up to me. I take a chance and ask if he is Belle's father. He says that he is. "You must be very proud." He gives a big grin and responds with a nod of his head.

As the ladies chip to the green, a woman approaches me and says,

"Not a very good day." I respond, "A Spring day at Machrihanish." Not realizing she is Belle's mother, and with one putt to go for the win, I say, "This match is over." Suddenly, she moves six feet away, and I realize who she is. She was probably concerned that I have jinxed her daughter. Fortunately, the putt goes in. Belle wins. With a hug from her "mum" she runs to her dad and all six feet of her jump into his arms.

15 WHISPER IN MY EAR

As I watched the Ladies' Scottish Amateur, I heard a voice in my ear ask, "How duss thi metch stend?" I turned my head to answer the question and saw an attractive forty-year old woman.

Rather than answer the question I asked, "Do you have a daughter playing in it?"

"Nooo, Aye played en ittt," she replied.

Oops! I wished I had not asked about her daughter. "I hope you played well," I said. I don't think a woman ever wants to be reminded of her age. I then told her how the match stood. "My name is Jim Wedge."

"Mine es Roslyn Bodate," she said with sharp eyes. It was obvious that my initial question about her daughter had not been well received.

"Enjoy the match," I said as we went different directions. I felt
bad that I had insulted the woman.

As coincidences happen, I ran into her at Westport Beach a few
weeks later. I was being a tour guide for a friend staying with me.
As we got to the gate to the beach, a woman with a Labrador was
coming out. Although dusk, I could see the outline of her face. As
she walked by I said, "Excuse me, aren't you Roslyn Bodate?"

"Aye," she responded.

"I'm the fellow who spoke to you at the Ladies' Amateur about
your daughter," I said.

"I knowww," she said. Her responses were rather short.

"Would you like to play golf sometime?" I asked.

"Surrrr, hoot," she came back.

"Here's my number. Give me a call and we'll play," I said handing
her my phone number.

Roslyn called a week later. "Helllo, thes es Roslyn Bodate, let's
play?" she said.

After finding out she liked to play early in the morning also, we set up a time for the next week. Meeting at the first tee at 7:30 we teed off. Roslyn has a wonderful swing. Being strong the ball goes a long way. Like many of the local women she is made for the outdoors. I'm sure she could chop a cord of wood without working up a sweat.

With our drives in the fairway we headed out. Not much was said as we played our shots on the first few holes. "Good shot" or "nice putt" was about the extent of the conversation. On number 4, a one hundred twenty-five yard par 3, she hit a wonderful 9 iron that stayed on the green even though the wind was behind us.

"How long have you lived here?" I asked.

"Ell my life. Myyy family hes e farm uppp thi road. I'm en artist. I paint withhh oils," she replied. It was nice to have someone to play with on an early morning round. By the time we got to number 14 the sky was blue with the sun shining brightly. I'm not sure why eighty degrees here feels warm, but it does.

"Can you believe this day?" I asked.

"Aye, et's e purfecttt dayyy te shaggg en thi grass," she said.

"Aye," I replied not knowing what she meant by "shag." I could see by the quizzical look on her face she realized I didn't understand.

A week later I asked Billy what "shagging in the grass" is. "Jimmmm, ere yuuu dafttt? It es e roustabout en thi gress."

"You would have thought I could figure that out," I replied. However, in the States all we shag are baseballs in the outfield during batting practice.

It is amazing how often in Scotland I have to ask a person to repeat what he or she has said because I don't understand. Between the Gaelic words and the Scottish words it is difficult for an American to catch on. Such words as braw, haar, smirr, peedle, gundy, flummoxed, hoot, wobbit, dwam, … are not in the American vocabulary. The Campbeltown speak is even more difficult to understand. Since this town is so isolated, the locals have a vernacular peculiar to this area. For example, a Campbeltown local might say, "Whet's fir dinner, hoot?" The translation is, "What is for dinner what?" Speaking very rapidly they will merge a three-syllable word into one syllable. It becomes unintelligible when a complete sentence is spoken. For example, "Urryewa-antin'somethun?" translates into "Can I help you?"

Roslyn Bodate and I are still playing golf. She still hits a big ball. She now talks a lot as we walk the course. I think we've solved most of the problems in the world. For all the golf we've played there has never been another sunny day. I'm sure if there is Roslyn will say again "et's a purfecttt dayyy te shaggg en thi grass." She'll be surprised to find out that my vocabulary now includes that word.

16 GOLF AT THE DUNES

I told Hector McDonald while we were watching the Open that Bobby Blair and Ronald McFair were coming to Machrihanish. I suggested the four of us play at the new course, Machrihanish Dunes, designed by David McKay Kidd of Bandon Dunes fame. "Aye'll trey to du thet," he said. "Lit me look et me schiduuule."

I like Machrihanish Dunes. It is a nice change from Machrihanish Golf Club. Bobby Blair and Ronald McFair hadn't played it. There's a reason for that. Bobby had refused to play at the Dunes since it opened. "Et's nutt guulf with blind shutts, " he said. Similarly, he doesn't like Machrie on Islay, because you can't see the greens on your second shots. I don't agree with him. Golf is a game with a lot of misses and unknowns. Sometimes a thinly hit shot skips through a bunker onto the green. On the other hand, a ball hit perfectly off the face with the perfect sound might back off the green into a hazard. It's a game of inches. Sometimes the golf gods are just "messing" with you. Sometimes it's your mind that lets you down. I figure that a few blind shots on a course merely add to the unknowns. Golf is a game of bounces where the ball eventually finds the hole. It just doesn't always go your way. I said to Bobby, "The way we hit the golf ball, we might as well have blind shots."

On Tuesday, when they arrive for an afternoon knock around, I mention that Hector McDonald would like to play with us at Machrihanish Dunes. "How do you boys feel about playing one round at the Dunes?" I ask. "I played it last Saturday. The fairways have come in nicely in a year and, except for some fescue in the greens, they putt fine."

To my surprise and relief Bobby replies, "Thit sounds goot." Walking into the pro shop I ask Hector which day he can play. He says it would probably be the next morning. "I'll till yuuu whin yuuu commme en efter yurrr rounddd."

With the round over we head into the pro shop. Hector announces with a big grin on his face, "We ere playing et 8:00 A.M. et thi Dunnns. Therrr are firrrballs going out at 8:30. We need te be in frunttt of thimmm."

"But what about the weather?" asks Ronald. The forecast was for rain.

"I can't control the weather," the pro replies. I wish McFair wasn't asking about the weather. This was very nice of Hector to set up a golf game at another course.

With Ronald shaking his head, obviously still concerned about the weather, I say, "Should we go directly to the course and pay there?"

"Go te thi cuuurse. I heve it covered," Hector replies. I'm looking forward to the Dunes all the more now. What a nice guy.

Ronald, still flummoxed with the weather forecast for the next day continues, "Maybe we should do it when the weather is better."

"No, thae es thi unly timmm I cen playyy," came the reply from Hector.

In the clubhouse we order drinks. No one had won the match. We walked in after fourteen holes in a downpour. Thank heavens for downpours. Bobby was leading. Without completing the round, the bet was off. Still concerned about the next day's weather Ronald says, "I dun't knuu if Hector wes kidding or whither he wes serious ebout pleying." I just shake my head.

"No, Hector was serious, and he has arranged for us to play for free. That will be saving you one hundred and twenty-five pounds a man," I say.

"Aye," Bobby remarks.

McFair remains fixated on the weather. Before we go to dinner he checks the weather report on the "tellie." The forecast shows that the morning will be the best part of the day. After that, it is going to rain.

I get to the Dunes early the next morning to hit balls on the range. As I am finishing, Bobby Blair and Ronald McFair show up. They have never seen the Dunes before. Driving in is impressive with a beautiful stone halfway house situated at the end of the carpark. There is no clubhouse on the property yet. Instead, this small building is used as both a pro shop and a restaurant.

Soon thereafter, Hector arrives. After getting his bag out of the trunk, we walk to the first tee. It is actually quite a walk, four hundred yards up a sand dune. When we get to the tee, the highest point on the golf course, a light mist hits our faces as we look out at Islay in one direction and Northern Ireland in the other. The Irish Sea looks a little dark with the overcast skies, but hopefully the weather will hold.

"What a morning," I announce. "What could be better than a round at the Dunes with good company?"

"Whin do they arrive?" Hector McDonald responds dryly. He has known Bobby and Ronald for many years. Bobby played as his partner in county tournaments. Bobby was the better player. Hector was just a boy then. For them, the tables have now turned. The pro says, "Runaldd end I willl teke yuuuu two on en e besttt balll."

Bobby is still fighting a snap hook off the tee. He is always looking for the right driver. Unfortunately, the problem is not the club. Instead, the fundamentals are bad. He is still flipping his hands after impact. His body stays low as if he is chasing after the ball. He and I have our job cut out for us if we are going to win this game.

After a couple of holes, the mist clears, and the waterproofs come off. We have already walked up and down a few sand dunes, so our heart rates are up. With the long walks between the tees and greens I wasn't sure if Bobby and Ronald would be physically up to this game. I had told McFair it was easier to carry your clubs than bring a trolley because the ground is so uneven and hilly. He did not listen. He brought his electric trolley.

The trolley has become quite the sight as we play along. It not only has McFair's clubs and gear on it, but most of Bobby's also. As Bobby takes off his waterproofs, he asks McFair if he will take them. "I din't heve room fir thim in the baggg. I'll slide thim around the hindle." McFair now looks like a tinker. He is loaded down like he has all of his earthly belongings on that trolley.

"Ronald, da ya hive eny weterrr? I'm thirsty," Bobby says.

Ronald looks at me, as if to say, "Can you believe this?" He then hands him the water and watches in horror as Bobby does his best to backwash into the bottle. "I'm lik a fuuuuuuucking dromedary," he mutters. For some reason Bobby never hears the complaints or picks up on McFair shaking his head. Or perhaps he does and doesn't care.

McFair is becoming a sideshow with his bag continually turning on the trolley and then falling off. It has happened at least eight times so far. Each time McFair has to find a flat spot for the trolley so he can get the bag back on. Flat spots on this golf course are few and far between. It is a lot of work for McFair over and above just trying to play golf. With the uneven ground, the handle of the trolley twists at its base, which then tips the bag over. I keep my laughs to myself as he repeats the routine. "Ach aye sitt," he utters. I can't even look at Hector McDonald. If I do, we both are going to laugh uncontrollably.

The holes at the Dunes are beautiful. Bobby Blair and Ronald McFair seem to be enjoying the course. They are talking positively about it, noticing the wild look, the undulating fairways, and the greens set into dunes. It is one of the most natural courses in Scotland because the developers couldn't move any dirt; it is an environmentally sensitive area. Basically they mowed between the tees and greens and had a golf course. I am glad the boys are having a good time. The Dunes, as a second course to play, will be a good change for our regular matches.

Hector McDonald is as good a player as he is a teacher. I cannot believe how far his ball carries, as he comes out of the ground after impact. I am happy to see that. I don't think Bobby, who was a better player than the pro many years ago, is quite as pleased. As Bobby hits low hooks into the tall rough, Hector McDonald hits high power fades.

Bobby says to me later, "Whet goot es it thetttt Hector McDonald has e gammme? He hes nowhere te playyy egainst professsionels."

My response was quick and direct, "What could be more satisfying than playing at a high standard and that you can actually do what you are teaching?" Bobby didn't respond. He was probably thinking about his next hook.

We lose on the 17th hole. The pro has five birdies. He was at least three under par. Now on 18, the rain is starting to come down. At the halfway house, we eat a nice lunch and talk about the round. Bobby and McFair continue to praise the course. Later that evening I am surprised at dinner when they tell me in unison they will never play there again. "Ta muccch werkkkk," Bobby said. I could not believe my ears. A great course that they played for free with good company. I guess it is a hard walk: eighteen holes at the Dunes are like walking thirty-six at Machrihanish. I'll miss their company at the Dunes, but look forward to playing more rounds there with the pro.

17 STABLEFORD

The boys from Crieff are back for a knock around. It is a three-hour drive for them. I don't think I have ever played well after riding in a car that long. My back doesn't seem to get sore, but my body feels stiff. I can't complete the backswing. If I don't get a good shoulder turn, my shots are very thin and low to the ground. The club clanks on impact, which is not the sound you want to hear. However, with a good shoulder turn in the backswing I hit down on the ball with a square hit at impact. The sound is entirely different, as the club compresses the ball.

Ronald McFair is just back from a trip to America. It sounds like he had a great time visiting Chicago, St. Louis, Nashville, Memphis, New Orleans and Lafayette. He loved Chicago. "It es e butifilll cityyy. There wes e big game. Thi Texas Rangers wirrr pleying enother team. It wis cold, but I wes en shirt sleeves," Ronald goes on.

Bobby says that he has been on a trip also. "I took thi steem enginn trrain frim Fort William te Campbeltown with en artist I met en thi internit. I surprised her with thi overnight trep. Thi countryside wes beautifel. We hed e goot time."

"Will I get to see her?" I ask.

"Noo," he replies, "weee won'ttt be seeing echhh other egain." It must be difficult finding a good match on the Internet. Also, I think most women would like to know in advance that they are going on an overnight date. It must have been quite a shock to the lass, when she learned they wouldn't return until the next day. The poor woman probably wondered if she had been kidnapped. It isn't easy to be in the dating game at age fifty.

After lunch we head to the first tee. Today we are playing a Stableford format with full handicaps. The player gets one point for a bogey, two for a par and three for a birdie. The player with the most points at the end wins.

The playing conditions are perfect; so good that Ronald on the 7th tee changes into shorts. At that point I wish I had shorts on to enjoy the "barbecue weather." When the sun is up and unobstructed by clouds, the Scots don't tan. Instead, their skin gets bright red. They must have a vitamin deficiency. Upon leaving the tee, Ronald McFair declares, "I look like an extra for Bridge Over the River Kwai with peacock legs." He is quite a sight with his paper white legs.

The only negative in the round is the group in front of us that is holding us up. It turns out to be two fathers and their sons. One dad is an American and the other a Scot living in Southern California. I can only explain their slow play as either their having watched too much golf on television or they really don't care about the groups behind them. The pro knows who they are. He told us later, "The cleb es accepting enybudy who gits spunsered. Thiy'll eccept enyone; people who cen't play and dun't know thi gaaame. Thi etiquette es becoming worse end worse."

We finally get a stroke of good luck when, on number 10, they lose a ball and decide to look for it. They have no choice but to let us through. They act as though we are doing something wrong as we pass by. I smile and wave as I say, "Have a great day guys."

Apparently, the slow play, perhaps exacerbated by my commenting on it, has affected Ronald the most. Although he had said earlier that waiting "is goot for thi soul," he didn't mean it. What he really meant was something like "Thes es slow es shettt trickling uut of thi neck of e bottle onnn e frosttty mirninggg." On 18, after the customary handshake, he announces, "This runddd of golf wes awfil. Et wes too slowww." Ronald saw the round differently from me. Actually, his comment surprised me. I had quite enjoyed the round. With the sun beating down, good friends, and playing well, "if et wes any better it wulddd be too goot."

The next morning we meet at the first tee at 8:45. I had told
Bobby the previous day that we should adjust the handicaps, since
I had won by a large margin. To my surprise, however, Bobby the
six is now a thirteen. Ronald has gone from fifteen to eighteen,
which is fair. My handicap has been reduced from nine to seven. I
had to laugh when I heard the new handicaps. I only meant
McFair's handicap should be increased. I didn't expect to end up
with the lowest handicap.

It is a warm windless morning. Islay and Jura look like you could
touch them. The Irish Sea has turned into a quiet lake. The
skylarks dart around the sky as they sing. This time I have my
shorts on to enjoy the barbeque weather.

The round goes well, however Ronald is tired. He and Bobby
shared a room in Belachunty at the Argyll Hotel where the bed
squeaked and the snoring was constant. We're probably too old to
share a room. There is nothing worse than listening to someone's
snoring while trying to sleep. When I've shared a room in the past,
I found myself trying to wake up the noisy roommate. If hitting
the headboard didn't work, I'd then throw a pillow or two. It never
seemed to work. The snoring sleeper would turn over and
continue snoring. At some point in life it is time to stop sharing
rooms on golf outings.

Bobby must have slept better than his roommate. He plays well
and wins the match. It is amazing how happy we are when we play

well. It is like life doesn't get any better than this. It is important to enjoy it for the fleeting moment, because it doesn't seem to last long. Almost as quickly as you think about your good play, it's gone. Bobby for the moment is almost giddy.

With the last putt holed on the 18th Bobby hurries to the pro shop. He announces that he is the winner. Hearing this, as I walk in, I add, "I had to give him shots." Hector gets a good laugh out of that. Bobby assures me that after lunch the handicaps will change again.

At the first tee in the afternoon, we learn of the new handicaps, "Jimmm es e tennn, Ronald es en eighteen end I'm e twelvvve," Bobby announces. I thought this was more reasonable. He is a good player. My only hope of winning is Bobby's wild driver. If he starts hooking it, I'll have a chance.

Ronald McFair and Bobby Blair are taking a buggy (an electric cart), so I guess I will too. I don't want to run to keep up with them. Additionally, since these boys aren't used to operating a buggy, I want to be able to stay out of harm's way. Hector McDonald's carts don't have a governor on them. With gas engines these are the fastest EZGO carts I've ever seen. Ronald and Bobby are like kids on the Autobahn at Disneyland. Their driving is very stop and go. The buggy swerves as they approach the narrow bridge spanning the Machrihanish Burn. It looks like even money they will end up in the stream below. To my surprise, the buggy straightens out as they reach the bridge and they get to the other side without wrecking. As they power it straight up the hill to the second green, I wonder if "buggies" should even be on this very hilly old golf course. Someone is going to get hurt. I don't think Old Tom Morris would have approved of this.

Ronald starts complimenting Bobby on his play. "Yurrr old swing es beck," he says. "Yuuu ere starting te hittt et on thi button," as a well-played shot is lofted into the air. "Gitting much closer," he adds. "Yurrr putt wes more difficult thenn mine." The positive input is helping Bobby. He is hitting the ball better. He is starting to think he can beat me. A competitive man by nature, it is obvious he wants to win. With him now thinking that he can, he may just do it. Oftentimes the difference between a good shot and a bad shot is the mindset. If you think you can play a good shot, it is more likely to happen. Success at golf is, in large part, believing you can do it.

I was hoping Ronald would win our third match, so I am trying to help him by being the self-appointed rules committee. On the 7th he plays a ball out of the rough that is not his. I suggest he go ahead and play his ball without a penalty. I think this is fair, considering Bobby has taken a drop on the 2nd fairway from a sanded divot. However, Bobby quickly responds, "That would be cheating Jimmm."

I remark, "I thought that would be the gentlemanly thing to do."

"Oh no," Ronald McFair interjects, "that would be against the rules. 'Thi noblest of God's creatuuures es en honest mannn.'" That is fine with me; you can only do so much to help the other guy. So much for me being the rules committee. Ronald gets no points on this hole.

Unfortunately for Bobby, that ruling comes back to bite him on the 10th hole. After two good shots on the par 5, he is fifty yards short of the green in a bowl in the fairway. I am even closer to the green in another low spot. I am very surprised when the boys' buggy speeds up to the precise spot where I hit my ball. Bobby quickly sizes it up and hits a ball, as I sit in my buggy to the side of the play. Parking in front of the green and not seeing another ball around, I walk over to the bunker thinking that perhaps it rolled in. When it is not there either, I walk to the green to see if Bobby has played the wrong ball. Sure enough on the green lies a PRO V1 black 4 with the name "Jim's 4-ball" printed on it.

Turning around I say, "This is my ball." Bobby turns his head back down the fairway and starts walking. He quickly finds his ball twenty yards behind where he had hit mine.

"Myyy compititivvve instincts ere gonne tootally," he responds, realizing he hadn't even looked at the ball to identify it as his. With the previous ruling Bobby made on Ronald's ball, he now takes a two shot penalty resulting in a double bogey seven and no points.

Unfortunately, I am still hitting some thin shots. I hit a "Sally Gunnell" on the 14th; the ball is one foot off the ground and moving fast. Apparently, Sally was an Olympic runner who was fast but not the prettiest "gelll." In Scotland on links courses these shots usually go as far as a well struck-shot. The ball finds the green resulting in another par and two points. Bobby announces on 16 that the match is over because I have so many points. We keep playing in and fortunately I make a bogey putt on 17 for one point. Thinking the match has ended and not concentrating as well, I miss a four-footer on 18 for a bogey and get one point instead of two. I played as well as I can for a 76. I am surprised to learn at dinner, when the boys pay off the bet, that the points earned are 40 for me, 39 for Bobby and 38 for Ronald.

I guess the match wasn't over when Bobby made the earlier announcement. This is part of why we like the game so much. Until the last shot is in the hole, it is unclear who the winner is going to be. For the player who is behind there is always a glimmer of hope. For the player leading, oftentimes he is holding on for dear life trying to get to the clubhouse.

Hector McDonald joins us for dinner at the Tandoori Restaurant. "End whooo won thi afternoon rouunnd?" he asks. "Jimmmm," came the reply from Bobby. The pro gives me a quick nod of his head. We settle into a nice dinner of tandoori chicken and nann bread. We all enjoy the meal.

18 THE LESSON

As I look back, I've spent a lot of money on new golf clubs trying to improve my game. Somehow I thought new equipment would make a difference. Perhaps a new driver would correct my snap hook. A sand wedge with new grooves would be just the thing to improve my sand play. Certainly my iron play would be better with a player's club—these cavity-back clubs are far too forgiving. Unfortunately, while spending money on equipment, I've spent very little on lessons. I can count on one hand the number of lessons I've had in my lifetime. Unfortunately, only one of the previous lessons I had actually helped me. The pro, Bruce Ashworth, who I golfed with growing up, and who became a star at the University of Houston, gave me a lesson years ago at the Dunes Hotel driving range.

"Jim, you have aimed to the right of the target all your life. Draw a line to the target with your feet parallel to that and you will be square to the target," he said. "Make sure your hips and shoulders are parallel to that same line." That one lesson made the swing so much better. I could now hit the ball farther and straighter. However, there were other problems with my swing that weren't changed. First, it was too upright with my hands separating from the body as the club went back. The swing was rerouted as it came down. I swayed back on the backswing. I had reached a plateau in my golf game years ago. My scores were in the low 80's only because I had a good short game. Like all golfers I would like to shoot in the 70's consistently. It is time to now take lessons.

Hector McDonald's description of the golf swing while we watched the Open made a lot of sense. This was somewhat of a surprise to me. Over the years I have resisted taking lessons because I have always thought I was not getting the whole story about the golf swing. For example, I could never understand in Golf Digest the instruction on how active the lower body needed to be. "Keep your legs moving," the articles would say, accompanied with a picture of Jack Nicklaus swinging. All that ever seemed to do for me was get me in front of the ball. The golf ball would then come out low. Jack on the other hand was hitting a two iron as high as my nine iron. He was doing something different. But I had no idea what it was.

Likewise, in the few lessons I had taken years ago, I was only getting part of the story. Keep your grip short, hit the ball first, pronate your hands going back, keep the left arm straight, keep your shoulders horizontal to the ground on the backswing, transfer weight to the right side, as if you are throwing a ball. These were some of the snippets I got. All this instruction did for me was create a slide and thin shots. I've never hit my irons on the face of the club. Instead, it has always been on the bottom of the club.

My last lesson was with a female pro, Suzie Maxwell, who had won two Women's U.S. Opens. I told her I wanted to hit down on the ball, that I hit too many thin shots. She was sure the problem was in the grip. She shortened my hands on the grip while making it more neutral. Trying that I still hit thin shots. At the end of the lesson, at least she had the honesty to say that she didn't know what I was doing wrong. After paying for the lesson, I walked away shaking my head.

In listening to Hector McDonald describe the golf swing, I feel like a light has finally switched on. I understand what he is saying. Stack and Tilt makes complete sense. All of a sudden I can see, for example, what Sam Snead is doing in his swing. I am sure for Snead it was his natural swing. He didn't have to make changes. He stays over the ball while he swings around his left side with his shoulder underneath. His back is vertical at the top of the swing. If anything, it looks as though it has moved forward. Coming down his legs drive into the ball. He then rises up after impact as he moves forward.

After a morning round at Machrihanish, I come back for a lesson. Hector and I jump into a buggy and head to the practice area. To avoid driving on the golf course, he drives onto the beach. "Ifff wi gitt stuck, yuu'll heve te pussh," he says. I just look at him and then at the beach. The sand seems firm enough for our ride. As we approach the Machrihanish Burn from the beach, the sand is covered with rocks that have been left from the combination of high tide and flooding in the burn. Hector doesn't seem concerned about damaging his golf cart as we speed over the rocky ground. As we come into the practice area, I am surprised at how big it is. Somewhat hidden from the 2nd fairway by sand dunes, I did not realize what was here.

Hector has a lot to change in my swing. At address I have a baseball grip. I re-grip the club as I forward press. Taking the club back my hands actually go down, as I try to keep the club low to the ground. Finally the club comes up too upright. The arms separate from the body. The shoulder turns minimally. The left arm collapses. The weight goes back to the right side. On the down swing it slides forward. I chase after the ball, staying low to the ground in the follow through. I realize this is going to be a painful process, but I'm ready to make the change. Golf will be so much more enjoyable for me if I can do it.

He first works with my grip. "Yuu need te change your grepp to e Vardon grippp," he says.

"The only reason I went to a baseball grip was because my thumb hurt too much," I reply.

"Yuuu need te hold thi clubb like this," he demonstrates by gripping the club. His left hand was in a very strong position with his right hand neutral. "Huldd thi cleb tight, so Aye cen't pell et out of yurrr hendss," he said. "O'Grady seys thi bird's head should pop off es yuuu squeeze." That also was new to me. "Keeep yurrr riiitttt thumb in close. Dun'tt extindd et," he continues. It is amazing how awkward the club feels in my hands all of the sudden. Also, my left thumb hurts a bit with the right hand on top of it but I wasn't about to tell Hector about the pain.

"I wanttt yuuu te stay over thi ball es yuuu swinggg," the pro says. Now that is not easy to do when you have swayed all your life. I felt very constricted trying to take the club back in one piece. I can see, however, that Hector is a very patient man. He is going to make these changes in my swing one at a time. At address my hips are in flexion. As the swing goes back, the hips change to extension with my right leg almost straight and my back vertical to the ground.

On the takeaway, I have always kept the club low, as if dragging it back. It made the swing oblong instead of circular. Hector wants the club to come up naturally. The swing then becomes round, and in that position my lifting the club is eliminated as the shoulders turn. Unfortunately, I am so used to taking the club outside, I feel like I'm never going to get to the ball.

I take a couple of swings with the same result. "Ohhh," says the pro as my shot goes a foot off the ground thirty degrees to the right. The balls disappear into the long grasses. I apologize to Hector for another lost ball. Trying to get my backswing to naturally go up, Hector put an electric cart behind me. "Tryyy thi backswing slowly weth outt hetting thi bugggy," he says. I'm not sure I can keep from hitting the cart. It takes quite an effort to avoid it in my backswing. At this point I'm wondering if change is good. The new swing feels anything but natural. My shots now are awful. Even with the awful shots, however I have not lost hope.

It is obvious I am going to have to hit a lot of balls if I'm going to end up with a better swing. I head over to the Machrihanish Dunes practice area after the lesson. I will make the adjustments slowly. A starting point is the grip. Changing to a Vardon grip with a strong left hand from a baseball grip is big in itself. Hector McDonald also wants my backswing to be a lot flatter, but I'll have to work gradually to get the club on plane. If I do it all at once, I'm going to keep hitting low "worm burners" to the right. It is a good thing that the Dunes practice area is very secluded, so I can make swing changes in privacy.

It turns out I am not the only person changing my swing. It is the last day of the PGA Championship at Atlanta Athletic Club. Tiger has a new swing coach, Sean Foley. He has missed the cut. During the first two days of the tournament, I'm not sure if he hit a fairway. Nevertheless, he is remaining positive in his interviews. I have to laugh at the way writers and commentators have written off his comeback. Colin Montgomerie, who is announcing, speaks quite authoritatively about Tiger's demise and how awful his play is. "He will never get it back." Colin is so full of himself it is hard to listen to his commentary. I am amazed how fast golf announcers in general write Tiger off when he is down. I have every confidence in the world that Tiger will win more Majors. Likewise, I am equally convinced that Colin Montgomerie never will.

19 A ROUND AT CARRADALE

As I walk in the pro shop, Hector McDonald greets me. "Howww err thi changes cumingg along?"

"Slowly, but I think I can do it," I reply with a positive tone.

"I heve thi efternuun ufff. Let'ss goo to pley gulff et Carradale Golf Club".

"I would love to."

"I'll pick yuu uppp et 3:00."

As I would expect, Hector is right on time picking me up. He is a very organized and punctual man, evidenced by the way the inventory in his pro shop is meticulously folded and stacked in cubicles. Carradale is twenty miles away down a two-lane track.

Actually it is sometimes one lane. Because of that, I wish I were driving. The signage "Blind Summit" at the top of a hill pretty well explains the uncertainty of this road. You can only hope a lorry is not coming from the other direction. The road is windy and steep. I'll just hang on and hope for the best.

"Fiona hes gone te Glasgow fir e couple of days," he says.

"What did she go for? Did she go with some girlfriends?" I ask.

"I dun't knowww. Shee tild mee, buutt I wesn't listning." The pro listens the same way I do when Lydia speaks. I think it is just a habit. I'm going to try to pay better attention when she talks.

I have been to the 1st green at Carradale Golf Club numerous times. It's a par three straight up a hill. The green is the highest point of the golf course. The view is magnificent from there. Across the Kilbrannan Sound is the island of Arran. To the right is Ailsa Craig. To the west is the Mull of Kintyre. It a three hundred and sixty degree view. However, it is very exposed to the elements. The trick is playing the golf course on a windless evening. Luckily, we are doing just that.

An elderly couple on 9 watches the pro tee off on the par 3 1st hole. They seem to be in awe. He's a big strapping man who hits the ball with a lot of power. He hits a nice shot that lofts into the air. It needs to, because of the elevated green. His ball finds the green; mine does not. The next hole looks out over a meadow with a medieval rock wall running across the fairway. On the 3rd hole Hector says, "I'mmm going te gitt e hole en onnne." I'm thinking what an odd remark. Using a three wood the ball takes a towering flight, hitting 10 feet short of the pin and ending up 10 feet beyond the pin. There was no hole-in-one, but it came very close. Perhaps the pro knew what he was talking about. His swing is right out of <u>The Stack and Tilt Swing</u> Mike Bennett and Andy Plummer. It is nice to know Hector can actually do what he is teaching me. It gives me more hope.

As I knock in a putt, Hector says, "Bobby, seys ya er thi besttt putterrr hes evir seen—even better than Bobby Locke."

"I don't think so. If you make one putt, Bobby thinks you're the best, because it's not his ball going in," I reply. When someone tells you you're a good putter, it becomes difficult to get the ball in the hole. I proceed to miss a lot of putts after the pro's comment. The greens are not bad considering the greens crew is just one person. There are some rough patches, but the putts roll well. In fact, if you are above the hole, it is possible to putt off the green. The greens are so small that you can play your shot off the hills behind them and the ball comes back onto the green.

Hector McDonald then shows me Stack and Tilt with the driver. "Meke the widge with yurr hands end puush out yir hips towerd thi targit. Since youuu heve ferther ta go, with thi bell forwrd, ya

cen now git to it." I try it on the course. It makes sense, but I can't
do it. It seems as though on the backswing with the hips forward I
slide back to make the backswing. Obviously, I'm missing
something. It is going to take some time to figure out. Hector
watches my swing during the round. Instead of making
suggestions, he lets me enjoy the golf. I'm sure he'll have plenty to
say at the next lesson.

We head to the Carradale Hotel for dinner. The meal is excellent.
Hector orders a rib eye steak. I decide on the monkfish and
mussels. Our talk continues on golf.

"Seve, din't knooow muuuch abutt thi swing. It wes just natural fir
him. En 'is chips he gitsss low which increased thi dynamic loft
end he hit thi baaall higggh end soft. He din't understand whet it
meant to take thi club inside. He shulddd heve stayed with
Leadbetter. Leadbetter prior to O'Grady got him swinging goot.
At thi nixt Masters efter taking lessons from O'Grady, Seve's
caddy came over to Leadbetter end said you've got to see this.
Seve is hitting it everywhere. Leadbetter wint to thi range, saw thet
Seve wes nooot doing enything he showwwed himm. Leadbetter
walked away niver te teach Seve egain."

"I've got a Seve story," I say. "At the Masters, Ken Green and
Seve were playing together. On the 2nd fairway, Green hit it into a
crosswalk in front of the green where the grass was matted down
because of the rain. He asked for a drop. Seve said no. An official

arrived and agreed with Seve. As luck would have it, I was on number 10 when Seve hit it into a crosswalk there. He, of course, wanted a drop. Green said no. The official who arrived said he could have a drop. Green said he wanted another official. A second more senior one arrived and said Seve didn't get to drop out of the crosswalk. Smoke was now coming out of Seve's ears. Seve played from the bad lie. Ken Green is one of the few people who would have stood up to Seve."

Ken Green was a sight for sore eyes that day. He had nothing but the color green. Each piece of his outfit was a different shade of green including his glove and his shoes. Going down number 2, I heard an elderly patron say to her girlfriend, "Doesn't that boy have a wife?" Although not the best dressed, he wasn't afraid to protect the field that day.

On our way home we stop at Darrell McGregor's house, a seventy-three-year-old local Carradale banker, who has recently built a house overlooking Davaar Island. He had asked us to come by after speaking to us at the Carradale Golf Club. Darrell looks like he has been wrestling a bear. With a bald spot on the top of his head, the hair he does have is pointed every direction.

"Wout ya likee e coffee or e wee dram?" he asks.

"No thank you. I have been 'on the wagon' for twenty years," I reply. Darrell looks at me like I am nuts.

"How abut a springgg weterr?" he replies.

"That will be fine."

McGregor brings in the coffee for McDonald and water for himself and for me. "I thought ya wes going ta heve e coffee? I'llll be ep ell nightt," the pro says to Darrell.

"I diciidid to heve spring weter. Look. Here es e painting ef thi schoonir Carradale. End look hire es thi Campbeltown," Darrell explains. He sits in his easy chair, looking quite disheveled, as though he needs a lady in the house. Darrell divorced his wife a few years ago. Although the house is in perfect order, McGregor looks a bit lonely. He is a really nice guy. He talks to us about golf, Carradale Golf Club, a competition Hector McDonald played against another pro there, and the list goes on.

Then he changes the conversation to tablets, a Scottish candy made mostly of brown sugar. "Wut ya likee e teblet?" he asks. Being the good guest and fond of tablets, I say yes. Darrell brings in a home brew of tablets. We all have one. He explains how he cooked them. It actually was the smoothest tablet I've ever had. McGregor says it is all in the beating. Tablets taste like they are pure sugar.

It is getting late and we want to go, but Darrell obviously doesn't want us to leave. The conversation was never going to end. As we stand up, Hector makes the mistake of commenting on a golf club Darrell has by the fireplace. "Waittt," he says. "I em going te git thi clebs I wonnn thi chempionshipp withh." Darrell hurries off and comes back with some old persimmon woods. "Hirrr they ere," he says. We comment on them for a few minutes and then make headway to the door as McGregor continues his stories.

As we drive home, Hector turns to me and says, "I shuldn't iver picked up thi gelf clubbb." It is a nice evening but now very late. I get home at 10:00 P.M. I am happy to see that Lydia, although worried about my whereabouts, has not called the Strathclyde Police to report a missing person.

20 A LONGER LESSON

Even if I sound like a local now, there is a lot of conversation I still don't understand. With a golf lesson scheduled at 10:30, I tee off at 7:30. As I get to number 13, I wave to the boys in the "Sweeps" who are on the 3rd hole. They are probably wondering why I am not playing with them, since they invited me yesterday. On the other hand, they're probably glad since I won last week. No matter; I have a lesson to go to.

Opening the pro shop door, I see Fiona behind the counter. In my best accent, I say "Allloo."

"Goot merninggg, Jimmm. How wess et?"

"Aye rawwww winddd et isss," I reply.

"Thetttt et es," she comes back. "Nowwww Hectirr, yuuuu boyss well bi done by 12:00, ehhh. I hevvvv swimming."

"Nooo prublemm," Hector says as he gets his video and teaching aids ready.

The wind is howling by the time we get to the practice area. Hector has me hitting into the wind, which is a good idea. Hector, who obviously has been thinking about this lesson for some time, gives me instruction on how to finish my swing. My normal swing chases the ball with my body staying low to the ground. Hector wants me to come out of the ground like Keegan Bradley or Tiger Woods. With so many thoughts going through my mind—arms tight to the side, only move the arms when my back turns, left arm twenty degrees in when it's parallel to the ground, right leg straightens, left leg bends—my balls are going wide of the target. The thirty-mile per hour breeze blowing to the sea adds to the random ball flight. A fade moves more. I finally notice Hector McDonald looking at the ground once. "Risssst e momentt, Jimmmm," he says. You never want your teacher looking at the ground questioning whether the pupil has any chance of improving. I'm sure he wants me to rest in hopes that fewer balls will be lost in the rough.

As it gets closer to 11:45, I remind Hector of Fiona. "Littts pickkk epp thii balllls," he says. In tandem we quickly grab the balls using plastic tubes. The return buggy ride crosses over the 2nd and 17th and then directly up 18. For idle chatter I say, "Maybe I'll take up swimming like Fiona. That has got to be a good work out." Hector with a wide grin on his face replies, "Shisss nett swemmming etssss slemmming. Shisss doingg weitttttts." I am surprised at that. I guess she wants to get stronger by lifting weights.

As Fiona passes us as she heads for "weitttttts," she says, "Jimmmm, I'llll siiii yuuuuu whinnn I cummmm beckkk." Now how is that possible, I ask myself? I am already an hour and a half into the lesson. I plan on leaving soon, especially after being blown around in the practice area. "Jimmmm, cummmm entoo meeee efffice," Hector says as he loads his computer with the video from my lesson. Stopping the video six different times he shows me positions and then prints copies. The pro hands me the printout and tells me to write reminders on them. He goes through each page while I write notes. With that finished, he pulls a training aid out of his briefcase: a black pillow the size of a headrest. Putting it under his arm he shows me with a backswing how far the right arm is to stay from the body. The pillow stays right there. If I had tried it, the pillow would drop to the ground as the club went up. He then grabs a cut down golf club and swings with his head against the wall. McDonald reminds me that he has already given me a two-foot club, so I can do the exercise at home. Then without the club he repeats the same exercise. He reminds me that I should be able to take the club away without hitting the wall.

With that finished, he asks me what I would like to drink. We go outside to sit on the heavy wooden bench next to the front door of the pro shop. While I drink my Coke, Hector goes over the copied pages one by one repeating what he has said and what I have written down. I can see in the clubhouse the "sweep boys" having whisky and beers and looking our way. I'm sure they are having a good laugh as they watch the two of us sitting on the bench, as though we are waiting for the next bus to nowhere. "Oh, here comes Fiona," I say. I can't believe it. She was right. Another hour has gone by.

"Now how could Fiona lift weights in that short of time?" I ask.

"Netttt weitttttts," Hector says. "Shiii gettts 'weighed.' Thiiiii gittt tegithirrr en wighhhh enddd sepppert eichh etherrr onccce e weeeek. Etssss ayeee slemmmming clesss."

With Fiona now coming at us, and wanting to say the right thing, my brain quickly goes through possible things to say. She is now on us. I had better say something, "Fiona howww deddd et go?"

Shaking her head in the negative she replied, "I'mmmm thi semmme weitttttt."

"Maintenance es gootttt. Yuuuuu wonttttt losss weight every week." She gives me a blank stare and appears to have no idea what I'm talking about.

I've seen that look from her before. Two weeks ago, she and I were partners in a "greensomes" tournament in which you alternate shots after the best drive is picked. On number 9, the ladies' tee is one hundred and fifty yards in front of the men's out in the dunes. Walking toward the fairway from different angles I had no idea her tee shot was the same distance as mine. When I said to her to hit my ball, she gave me a similar piercing stare. I didn't understand the reason for the stare, until she had picked up her tee shot opposite mine. I should have been playing her ball into the green. "Fiona, I'm very sorry. We played the wrong ball," I said. If looks could kill, I would have been dead.

With Fiona back in the pro shop, Hector ends the three-hour lesson. I can't believe how much effort he is putting into improving my game. I figure, if he cares this much, I am not going to let him down.

21 THE VIKING CLASSIC

After playing in the Tuesday "Sweeps" as a 6 handicap and winning the money, I've become a hot commodity for future events. In the "Sweeps" everyone puts in two pounds and plays off their handicap. I should have had better judgment and not won the round. Instead, I am now in demand for team competitions.

Malcolm McSwain asks me to join his foursome in the Viking Classic. I want to say no, but can't. Malcolm is one of those guys you don't say no to. His memory is quite long. After I accept, I find out the format: the first six holes one score counts, the next six holes two scores count, and the last six holes three scores count. Although each player gets his full handicap, this is a difficult format. The last six holes will be brutal with three scores being used.

When Malcolm asks me to play, he said, "Jimmmm, heve yuuu

evirrr ceddied? Ere teem ess thi Caddy Lads. I thuttt aye bitterr make surrrr yuuuu've caddied."

Not sure why it makes any difference whether or not I have caddied before, I answer, "Yes I caddied at Glasgow Gailes for a pro in a qualifying round for the Senior Open at Troon. After he failed to qualify, I caddied for him at the Machrihanish Open, which he won."

Malcolm is relieved with my response. The team can keep the name Caddy Lads. "Gooottt, et ess twelve pounds fifty to play," he continues. A man of thrift and to the point, I give him the poundage, and the foursome is set for the competition.

The day of the Viking Tournament arrives. I pick the team up at the White Hart Hotel, where they've started with a few beers. The boys are in a jovial mood. They are excited as they talk about our chances of doing well in the tournament. Although Campbeltown was sunny and bright, it is now overcast and gray at the golf course. When we start, the wind is down, which is a nice change from the week before.

Watching the group in front tee off, I'm reminded we are playing from the white championship tees. These tees are placed farther back and often, as is the case at the 1st, at different angles to the fairway than the regular tees. Some of the tee boxes are off by themselves on dunes. The course is tougher from these tees. The

1ˢᵗ hole is difficult anyway, and now it is more so. The drive has to carry more of the beach to hit the left side of the fairway, where the ball will run. I get a good drive, but aim at the bunkers right. I don't want to start on the beach. With a light breeze into our face I'm left with a three wood into the green. The ball finds the green to my relief. I two putt for par. The Caddy Lads are off and running.

Over the next five holes, it is relatively easy to post one score. Starting on the 7ᵗʰ hole it becomes more difficult. We now have to use two scores on each hole. Additionally, it is the number one handicap hole; it is a long par 4 which doglegs right over a hill with the green hidden at the bottom. After a good drive, I put my ball in the long grasses below the rise as a result of a thin hybrid shot. I never do that. However, standing over the ball, I have a negative thought, second-guessing whether I can clear the hill. Rather than stepping away and catching my breath, I give it a go. It is a thin low shot. Next, with a relatively good lie in long grass I hit a nine iron on my next shot onto the green, but end up two putting for a disappointing bogey. Malcolm and Willy McLeish, another former Captain of the Club, get pars, which adjust to birdies with their handicaps.

I proceed to par holes 8 through 12. But starting at 13, we have to use three scores on each hole. The 13ᵗʰ is tough without any wind, but we were now playing into the wind. Eddie Farmer tees off first. As his club hits the ball, his left leg kicks sideways three feet off the ground as he staggers to keep his balance. It is a swing all its own. Unfortunately, it is not very effective. The ball is a low one which lands in the long grass one hundred yards off the tee. He hits a provisional, which unfortunately is a repeat of the first.

McLeish, who plays a big hook as always, tees his ball as high as Chi Chi Rodriquez, which puts the ball entirely above the club head. He is a former student of Hector's, however he decided "et es too much too think about" and gave up the lessons and the method a year ago. With a big swing he hits it hard. The hook snaps into the left rough in deep grass. You can never trust a hook, especially with the wind blowing right to left at thirty miles per hour. Malcolm was next. With a nice drive in the fairway we have one ball in play. I was last to tee off and in the fairway. With two balls in play and three needed for a score I hit a poor chip and get a bogey.

The 14th hole isn't any easier. It should be called the Long Hole. It is a very long par 4. With repeated undulations in the fairway the second shot has to get up a steep slope in front of the green. Most balls end up short of the green. The wind is still hurting the tee balls.

Eddie has a repeat of his shot on number 13. His leg kick in the air is getting the same results. He never comes out of flexion, which causes him to stagger on his follow-through as he tries to get extra distance. I've told him how Hector McDonald has helped me.

Eddie, in the twenty-five years he has played at Machrihanish, has never had a lesson.

With the wind over our left shoulder, Willy puts his ball in the left rough. Malcolm and I are in the fairway. No one reaches the green, but my ball is only ten feet short after a well-hit three wood. After a poor chip, which is ten feet short, I knock the putt in for a par. The other boys get two bogeys. We all get shots thanks to our handicaps, so we're one under for the hole.

It is more of the same coming in. I chip up on the 15th for a par. Before we hit our drives on 16, Malcolm pulls out his whisky flask with four shot glasses. Malcolm comments that it is a little watered down "itherwisse ets herddd en yurrr throattt."

"I thutt et wes e letttle different," responds McLeish. Obviously, he doesn't use water.

"Jimmmm, yuuuu preblyyy din't went one," Malcolm asks.

"Thanks anyway," I come back. The whisky should mix nicely with the lagers they had on the 13th tee. Perhaps the alcohol will smooth out their game.

To my surprise their games don't change. The whisky has not helped. At the 16th, Farmer is lost in the long grass. McLeish is out to the right in long grass. The team is coming apart like a cheap suitcase. I hit the green and two putt. The 17th hole, although only three hundred fifty-six yards from an elevated tee, is the longest short hole in the world. With the wind in our face I'm only one hundred thirty-five from the pin. My hybrid, which is a 185 club, hits short of the pin and runs over the green. However, the putt goes in for a birdie. If it hadn't hit the pin, it would have been ten feet past the hole.

The 18th is into the wind. Eddie tees off first with a drive that goes thirty yards into the grass. McLeish snaps his drive out of bounds. Malcolm and I both get pars with ours, and the third score we post is a double bogey. Amazingly, with a little luck I've played the last six holes in par. As it turns out, our 131 team score places fifth which is good enough for a prize.

The problem with being the chauffeur is I have to wait for these boys to have some drinks in the clubhouse. The players who teed off early have had a two-hour head start in the bar. They are sloshed, as they try to cheer on Scotland over Serbia in World Cup qualifying. With the game tied, the drinkers seem to know a lot about football, as they berate the manager and the players. Their fervor doesn't help. It ends in a tie. A number of them are now "blotto."

Glen Tanker catches my eye, as he walks like a zombie trying to find a rag to clean up the glass of lager he has spilled on the table. Apparently, he likes spilling drinks because he spilled another full glass at the bar. I wasn't too concerned about his antics, until I learn that he is the next Captain of the Club. He spends more time at the bar than on the golf course. Hopefully, he'll do better as the Captain.

Rankin Rast, the fishmonger in Campbeltown, comes over to McLeish, rubs his baldhead and gives him a peck on the neck. That is enough for me. "Boys, if anyone wants to come with me, I'm leaving." Malcolm and Eddie accept the ride. For McLeish the evening is just beginning, so he stays. He is one of eight guys who leave for Turkey on Wednesday for an all-inclusive golf trip.

"Et's ternning mi ento en alcoholic," McLeish says. (As I write this a week later, the boys are still in Turkey, where the US embassy has been attacked by Muslims, which is a continuation of unrest after the killing of the US ambassador to Libya. I hope they keep their heads down.)

During our drive to town Eddie comments on the "good value" he got at Tesco earlier in the day. The gin for his wife and Jura whisky for him cost a total of ten pounds each.

"Did you get any bread Eddie?"

"No, Jimmmm, thettt es nett en miii diettt."

Letting them out at the White Hart, Malcolm says, "Jimmmm, willl keepppp thi same teamm nixt yirr."

"Malcolm, I can't wait," I reply.

22 THE CRIEFF BOYS RETURN

Bobby Blair's swing is in a state of flux. Like all of us he wants to improve. Instead of paying for formal lessons, he will ask for advice from Hector McDonald in the pro shop. With one suggestion from Hector, he thinks he has sorted out his swing problems. "Aye heve et now," he exclaims. If only it were that easy.

It is amazing how difficult it is to make even a slight change in a golf swing. Starting with the grip it isn't easy to do. Make your left hand "stronger" by putting it over the club and the grip feels awkward. Move the ball back a few inches in your stance and your swing bottoms at a different spot. Open a closed stance so you are parallel with the target and your balls go far to the left because the swing is still "over the top." The swing is normally a matter of compensation for the player. The secret is to eliminate that manipulation. Unless you are right on plane, adjustments have to be made so the ball goes on line. Hector is trying to get me on plane, so there are no adjustments.

It is obvious Hector has told Bobby about the progress I am making because I start getting e-mails from Bobby. The last thing he wants is to have to get shots from "simmm Emerican." He has commented about my swing improvement during our rounds together. And now he wants to know how it is coming along. I try not to give him too much information. I think the unknown will be good for him. The suspense must be too much, so he is now trying to find out from Hector McDonald.

Ronald McFair calls on Monday night. "Jimmmm we're coming downnn tomorrow."

"I've got a game Tuesday morning with the caddy masters. Ronald, do you know a gale is coming on Wednesday?"

"Aye," replies McFair. "Ya knoow Bobbby, hi wints ta seeee yuuu." Since Ronald was here two days ago showing his wife around, I'm surprised he is making the long drive back. Usually they come when the weather is perfect. From the looks of it Wednesday is going to have gale winds and rain. Bobby pretty much makes the decisions in that group. Hopefully they'll get lucky on the weather.

After the match on Tuesday with the caddies, we head into the clubhouse to have a drink. I am expecting that after a few drinks, Ronald and Bobby will show up. It isn't long after that they arrive. As they walk in there are a lot of hellos. Bobby then makes his entrance and says, "Jimmmmmmm Widggggg." I nod. It is a little awkward because I am sitting with the guys I just played golf with. With the Crieff boys standing around the table the loud conversation seems to go on and on.

Finally, one of them says to me, "Ye're pleyyingg weth es thes efterninnn, eh?"

They seem stunned when I reply, "No, I can't. I have to drop the car off at 2:00 at the mechanic. At 3:00 I have an appointment for a haircut with Mari which I can't cancel." I decided after Ronald McFair's call that I wasn't rearranging my schedule because Bobby made a knee-jerk decision to come to Machrihanish. "I would love to play thirty-six tomorrow, weather permitting, and eighteen on Thursday," I continue.

"Aye, Aye," comes the response. They then settle down at their own table.

After a few more minutes with the caddies and one more round of drinks they hurry to the bus stop to catch the bus back to Campbeltown. I then walk over to the Crieff boys and say, "I'll join you for dinner. Where are you eating?"

"Riitt here," comes the response from Bobby. The food at the Club isn't the best in the area. I should have asked where they were eating before I volunteered to join them. I think they like the clubhouse for dinner because they can walk from their Bed & Breakfast at the Warren. They avoid the risk of being stopped by the Strathclyde police after a few drinks and then driving home.

The boys are very talkative over dinner. I hear all the details of their afternoon match. It is probably more details than I care for. "Did you get any rain out there?" I ask.

"Aye, et starrrrtid es e smirrr on 11 end then ceme sidddweys on 16."

"I'm sorry to hear that. Are your clubs in the drying room?"

"No, thiy're beck et thi Warren, thi Bid end Breckfest wirre et," comes the reply.

"Have you seen the weather report?" I ask.

"Et looooks beddd fir temorrrew," Ronald says.

"That's a shame," I respond.

The next morning it is a torrential downpour. I decide to wash my clothes and clean up the house. My last houseguest left only a few days ago. He was not as neat as my first guest. The house is in a bit of a state. Lydia is arriving in a week, and I want the house to look perfect for her.

The phone rings at 11:00. It is Ronald McFair asking if I want to join them for lunch. "I'mmm hoping thi rainnn willll lit ep," Ronald says.

When I get out of the car at the clubhouse, the wind is bending the flagpole. It is dry but with far too much wind. The boys show up after me.

"Are you playing in this?" I ask.

"Arrrre yuuuu?" comes the response.

"No. That is too much wind for me." Looking outside the oystercatchers, instead of flying, are scurrying on the ground as the wind is too much for them, too. The Crieff boys agree.

"Jimmmm, whett sheddd we dooo," Ronald McFair asks. He has asked the right person. I'd been a tour guide the previous two weeks with two different visitors. As a tour guide, I took them each to the same sites. Even though I knew this group was not interested in doing anything but play golf, I say, "How about Dunaverty Rock, Columba's footprint, followed by the lighthouse at the Mull of Kintyre?"

"Noooooo wi neeed sumethingg insidde," Ronald McFair says.

There are not many buildings in this "wee toon" and not much to do inside. I sarcastically respond, "How about the Aqualibrium? You can start with swimming, then the fitness center, and after a cup of soup end with a book in the library."

Shaking his head and smiling from ear to ear, "Noooooo, Jimmmmmm, whettt shilddd wiii do?"

I clarify quickly that I am not part of "we." I have things to do. I was planning on "shootttting thi craaaw," as in disappearing, until dinnertime. "I don't know, Ronald," I say. "I am going to continue cleaning the house because Lydia arrives next week. I'll join you boys for dinner."

Ronald, looking a bit scuttered, says, "Okayyy Jimmmm, we'll seee yuuu et Chinese et 7:00 P.M." I am sorry to hear this, since I know McFair doesn't like Chinese. I try my best to talk them into the Royal Hotel for dinner, but Bobby says it is too dear.

"I'll be there," I say as I walk away.

Finally, we get a bright, sunny day on Thursday and head to the course. On the first tee Bobby turns to me and says, "End whatttt esss Misterrrr Widgggg mesquaraddding et tedayyy?"

"I'm a 6," I say, catching Bobby off guard. He is, for a moment, at a loss for words.

"I'mmmm e sixxxx tooo." Now who is masquerading? We throw up balls. I get Charles who is a 4. McFair is a 9. Bobby wants to play a Stableford. Charles and I object. Instead, we decide to play a two man best ball. Charles and I are now partners against Bobby and Ronald. During the first eighteen, Bobby has never played better. Charles and I ultimately win the last two holes to break even.

As we eat lunch in the clubhouse before our next round, I interject, "Charles and I want a rematch this afternoon against you two."

"Aye," says Charles.

"Nooooo, nooooo, wi'rrr threwwwing ep bells egainn," retorts Bobby.

"Really?" I ask, as Charles and I glance at each other. Apparently Bobby doesn't like his chances the second time around.

When we get back to the tee, Bobby goes to the pro shop to tell some jokes. With Bobby out of ear range I say to Ronald, "I can't believe Bobby doesn't want to have a rematch with the same teams."

"Jimmmm, aye knoww. Wi'll tilll Bobbby whin he comess outt thet wi threwww thi bells end hee gottt mi," says Ronald with a smile on his face. Almost immediately Bobby comes out of the pro shop. "Bobby, wi thru ep bells end I gottt yuuu," Ronald says.

"How cen thet beee myyy ball wisn't thirr," replies Bobby.

"Et wis thi closist tooo off thi threee," says Ronald. Bobby shakes his head, but there is nothing he can say or do to change this. The match is on.

Bobby and Ronald decide to take a buggy for the afternoon. I take one also. I tell my partner who is walking with an electric trolley to watch out if the other two are behind him. "They might run you over."

Our opponents lose six down with five holes to go. Charles and I put the hammer to them. Charles, a part-time taxi driver in Crieff, won the lottery a few years ago. It changed his lifestyle, so he now is able to play more golf. A very nice chap with a nice golf swing, Charles enjoyed winning the match early in the round. We exchange handshakes on the 18th green, as well as a few pounds. With a quick drink in the clubhouse, the Crieff boys have a five-hour drive back to Crieff. Rest and Be Thankful, the highest point in the Highlands on the A83 is closed due to a landslide, so with the detour at Inverary to Crinalrich the drive is longer than normal.

While we sit there, I ask if Charles helped with the driving. "Nooo, he'sss nott en thi insurance," Bobby interjects.

"Why not put him on so he can help?" I ask.

Charles answers, "I'mmm shurrr et wuldd bi easyyy. Nooo metter. I jest closee mi eyes en thi beck seat en gooo te sleeppp." He in particular has a long ride ahead. I've seen Bobby and Ronald drive before. I followed them in my car, as we drove to Montrose Golf Club. Their driving was stop-and-go along with a few wrong turns. I'm not sure their eyesight is the best. That is the only explanation I have for Bobby standing right behind me on the tee when I tee off.

THE BALL CHUTE

Walking to the first tee

The ball chute seems out of place.

With its shiny green enamel frame

It looks like it belongs in a factory not on the tee.

However, as my ball rolls down the chute

And it lines up behind the balls ahead

It now becomes clearer

How it has brought a semblance of order

To what might otherwise be simply chaotic.

We are third in line

There is no doubt where we stand.

The order of the balls in the chute has decided that.

With the next group off

There are now only two.

It won't be long before we can give it a go

I grab my glove and some tees so I'm ready

Our ball now is first in line.

Taking it out of the chute with some glee

The tee is now ours.

The shiny green frame has done its job

We're now ready for a game of golf.

23 ON THE CHEAP

The new swing is progressing, slowly getting closer to being on plane. My hands no longer separate from the body at the top of the swing. Since I am finally making progress, I'm enjoying the challenge. I now can compress the ball, and in so doing the ball goes a club farther. My shallow divot starts at the ball and continues four inches in front of it the way it should. The sound of the club hitting the ball is entirely different from before.

Bobby Blair and Ronald McFair are staying at the Warren B&B. While the boys are eating their full Scottish Breakfast, I'm hitting nine irons on the practice range. This is a nice change from not warming up. It is rather daunting standing on the first tee looking over the beach to the distant fairway. Every time I'm there, I ask myself why I haven't hit some balls. It will be nice to see if warming up makes a difference.

I get to the tee box before the others arrive. Sitting on the bench, I watch them pull into the carpark and hurriedly get their electric pull carts assembled and their golf bags in place. As usual, Ronald is walking very fast, as if he is late. He isn't, but that seems to be his manner. As he approaches, I ask, "How was breakfast?"

"Jimmmm, et wes splindiddd," Ronald replies. "Is Hector inside?" he asks.

"I'm not sure," I reply. Ronald ducks his head in the pro shop and learns from Craig that the pro is away.

On the first tee, Bobby tells us our "new" handicaps. The format again is Stableford. Ronald tees off first. He pops his drive up to the beach.

"Ohhhh nooo, Ronald," Bobby shouts. Bobby tees off next.

As we walk down the fairway, we can hear shotgun blasts from Machrihanish Dunes Golf Club. The grounds crew is killing more rabbits. Rabbits are digging holes and tunnels on both golf courses. I once stepped in one. Lying on the ground with my golf bag on my back I wasn't sure if I could get back up. My left foot was still in the hole with my knee aching. It was late evening at the Dunes. No one would find me until the next morning, if I had just lain there. Summoning all my strength, I staggered up, and to my surprise nothing was broken.

As the round progresses I am five points ahead in the Stableford. At the 10th both Bobby's and my ball are side by side on the fringe of the green. I am laying five having missed a shot in the long grass, and Bobby is laying four. "Jim, yuu goo ahead. I'll markk mi balll," he says.

"Bobby, I think you're away. I might be able to make this putt. I'm going to let you go first."

"Aye," he responds. Bobby misses it on the left edge for a par and two points. Having seen the line, I roll my ball in for a 6. I'm glad I didn't let Bobby talk me into going first. Seeing the line is the only reason I made the putt.

On the 11th my five-foot putt ends up four feet from the pin. Rolling the putt in for a two, I am now six points ahead of the others. At the 12th Bobby is grinding it out. However, he tugs his drive to the left. Although playable, he then proceeds to snap hook a ball out of bounds. With my feet two feet below the ball I hit a ball skinny but straight down the fairway. There aren't many level lies on this links course. With a wedge onto the green a par adds two more points.

The 13th hole has a false front in which the first thirty feet of the green rolls back to the fairway. The only way to get the ball on the green is to roll it on or carry your shot over the false front. I decided to go with an eight iron and roll it on. Although it was a bit chunky which helped with over spin, it ends up pin high at the top of the hill.

"Jimmmmm, thet is thi worsst shottt thet evir made thit green," Bobby shouts. I'm sure he is right, however it seemed to work. Another par adds two more points. Bobby gets zero after being in the tall grasses and then short of the green in three.

On number 14 Bobby hits another snap hook. He borrowed a Callaway driver from the pro shop. As stiff as that Pro Force shaft is, Bobby's shots shouldn't be going left. He'll be taking it back to the pro shop after the round. "I jist cin't git thi feeling," he calls out. I can't even watch the swing because it is faster than Zorro. This match has gone our way. On 15, a hundred and fifty-six yard par 3, I hit a 5 hybrid within four feet for another birdie. The match is over.

As we walk down the 18th, Ronald who is 69 says he's tired. "Jimmock," he says. "Life's short. Time flies. The older ya git thi festerrr et goes." His comment makes me think of a similar remark my dad made years ago. Walking up the 5th fairway at Paradise Valley Country Club in 1960 he said, "It seems just like yesterday I was your age doing things with my father." At age twelve I looked up at him incredulously not understanding the truth to his statement. Because it was so unusual for my dad to make a comment like that, I still remember the exact place we were. With time having gone by I finally understand what my dad meant in saying those words. I merely smile after Ronald repeats a similar expression.

Finishing the 18th we shake hands. Bobby and Ronald then chase up the hill to the pro shop. During the round, I had told Bobby about one hundred-pound trousers on sale for twenty pounds. Apparently the boys would like to get a pair. Unfortunately, with the sale starting a few days earlier, Bobby was disappointed his size was not there.

"He wints trousers en thi cheap," Ronald said. Trying on a pair, which was three sizes too big, he looks as though he has been on a starvation diet. The trousers fit like a tent. Fortunately, he doesn't buy them. Perhaps there will be another sale in the future. When you are looking for an item "on the cheap," it pays to be there when the sale starts.

24 KATHLEEN RUSSELL

Lydia has an appointment in Oban with the audiologist. Unfortunately a gale has blown in. Normally you don't venture out in a gale. However, Lydia has been waiting six weeks to get into the audiologist. Her hearing aid isn't working and she has patiently been waiting to get it fixed. We decide to give it a go and brave the gale.

As we head out of town I am not sure if we've made the right decision. When we first get a glimpse of the sea, it looks mad, as waves come in on top of each other. The sea spray is coming over the road. The leaves on the trees are being ripped off. The trunks look as though they cannot take much more as they bend from the force of the wind. The gale is soaking the trees in salt water from the sea. I am wishing we were in the safety of our house.

We stop in Lochgilphead at the Archway Gallery to find out how the artist Kathleen Russell is doing. She hasn't responded to our Christmas card. The last time I spoke to her last summer when we bumped into her at Stonefield Castle, she was awaiting the results of medical tests. She thought she had cancer.

As I walked in Wilma, the owner says with a big smile, "Yuuve nuttt binnn around."

"No, I left last June," I reply. As her assistant Mae walks in I ask, "How is Kathleen Russell doing? I didn't hear from her at Christmas time."

Their faces turn from jovial to ashen. They don't have to say anymore. "She died over the winter, Jimmm."

Visibly shaken I respond, "When?"

They are guessing it was late January or early February. She had "gone down very quickly."

With the news, I have lost interest in looking at art in the gallery. I thank them saying, "I didn't want to find out from her husband John when I went to Kilberry next time. Now I'll be prepared." Saying our goodbyes I leave the shop and get back in the Vauxhall.

Lydia asks what they said. "Kathleen Russell is dead."

"You are kidding," comes the response.

"No. Kathleen is dead." Lydia now realizes I am not joking. I proceed to tell her what I just learned. I start to feel numb and a sense of profound loss. Actually, I feel cheated. I am going to miss her. I didn't want our visits in Kilberry to end. I was looking forward to more time with this eccentric artist.

We first met Kathleen five years ago after dinner at the Kilberry Inn. I noticed a gallery sign next door to the Inn. "Lydia, let's check it out," I said. With a short walk and a knock on the door of the "Smitty," Kathleen's husband answered the door. A thin short man, John looked a bit disheveled in his wide wale corduroys and plaid flannel shirt, a scarf around his neck and his head of hair in disarray. He told us to wait in the gallery behind the house. While we waited, we looked at the art. It was amazing. Gouache used like oils, which she explained later was how she now painted because of a deteriorating hand condition. Gouache is a much quicker medium to work with. The artist finally walked in. I knew I was going to like this woman at first sight. With a longhaired fur vest over a large patterned paisley dress and a pipe in hand she asked, "Whett the fuuuuck yuuu winttt?"

"We'd like to see your paintings," I came back. After some chitchat, I told her which painting I wanted.

"Sorry, I'vvve given et to thi electrician. He hasn't binn able to

143

take et hommme yet becaussse he es werried hisss wiiife wun't like thi nuuud."

Kathleen and her husband met at the airport while awaiting a flight to Kenya. Kathleen was headed there to paint. John, a botanist, was collecting plant life. They fell in love on the trip. They struck up a conversation and decided to see Kenya together. A few years later, they married. Opposites clearly attract. While Kathleen is loud and petulant, John is soft spoken and mild-mannered. Kathleen is a large woman. John is small in stature. Upon his retiring as a curator of Kings College gardens in London, the pair moved to Kilberry, where Kathleen had spent time as a young girl. She continued her painting. John continued gardening by turning the acre behind the house into a beautiful garden.

After meeting her that first time, we made sure to visit on a regular basis. John always answered the door. I would say loudly, "I am looking for the artist Kathleen Russell." When she would appear from behind the door, I would continue, "I am looking for the artist Kathleen Russell."

Suffering from Asperger's Syndrome, Kathleen would reply with four letter epithets in a very guttural jumbled sound. "Litts guu sitt en thi gardenn," she would say. The garden has a stream running through it. With benches situated along the paths, she would pick one out. Sitting down, she would grab my hand to sit down also. She obviously liked men. The benches were only big enough for two people to sit on them. Lydia and John would stand at the end of the benches like the sphinx. It seemed a bit awkward with us sitting. Kathleen assured me they were fine. She did most of the talking. Every now and then I would ask a question and she would answer in a gruff but somewhat garbled manner. She would light her pipe and the talk would continue. Originally trained at Edinburgh University, her style has changed from realism to impressionism.

The last painting I bought from her is of John standing in their kitchen. It depicts a kitchen, which is a sight for sore eyes. With pans hanging from the ceilings along with clothes drying, pots stacked on the counter, stuffed animals on shelves, tall carved wooden camels from Africa, a painted ceiling with large bright flowers in the background, the impressionistic painting does a good job of capturing the actual scene. Kathleen and I worked out a trade. In exchange for a flowering Japanese almond tree now and a sweet pomegranate bush in the spring, I got the painting. The tree was provided a week later from Loch Fyne Nursery. The pomegranate was shipped in the spring.

The last time we met, we ran into each other at Stonefield Castle in Tarbert. We were there to look at Kathleen's art on display. She and John were spending a weekend celebrating their wedding anniversary. As we walked in, we bumped into John. Directing us outside we joined them for a drink. It was a sunny bright day as we sat on the back steps, so Kathleen in her plus fours and riding boots could smoke her pipe. With a whisky in one hand and the pipe in the other she looked like a character from a bygone era. After a long conversation on the steps the last thing she said to me went as follows: "We've had a great time this weekend. Why dun't yuuu fuuuuucking buuullshit damnn buyyy one ef my peintings?" Saying our goodbyes, that was the last time I saw Kathleen. As I look back, I wish I had bought a painting.

Ormsby Farms, up the road from Kilberry, provided a burial plot in their private cemetery for Kathleen. It is in the most beautiful setting off a single-track road with rock walls covered in black currant vines and wild roses. Lydia and I have stopped before and wandered through the graveyard in hopes of finding Kathleen's headstone. I thought I had gotten clear directions to the location of her grave. However, as of yet we've been unsuccessful in finding it. In any event it is a fitting location for an artist's burial plot with the Isle of Jura sitting in the sea to the West. She painted those "humps" on more than one occasion. She loved it there.

25 BILLY

There is a possibility of a squall today. I could wait and play in the "Sweeps" at 10:00 A.M. with the members. It is always fun to put a couple of pounds into the "pot" and then play your own ball. However, with any luck, if I play early I may miss the storm. I've decided to try to stay dry and play a quick early round.

Carrying only a few clubs in my carry bag, I head out. I have found I really don't need 14 clubs. If I'm in between clubs on a shot, I choke down on the grip to compensate. The wind keeps getting stronger as I play. Stack and Tilt is coming along. With my irons I'm starting to come out of the ground on the finish, which makes the ball go ten yards farther. Moving at a fast pace with waterproofs over my shorts, I enjoy the round. The mist stays the same. "Not a bad day" locals would say. However, it has the possibility of getting much wetter. To keep the bag light I have no umbrella.

Reaching the 11th, I realize the boys in the sweeps might cross over at the 6th to the 12th tee to get in quicker. As I get to the green, sure enough, two boys arrive on the tee. I am glad to see it is Billy, the Caddy Master and now philosopher, and a new member named Rankin. Now as a threesome, we are moving a little slower, but it is nice talking to Billy. Even though we are playing quickly I am making sure not to hit out of turn. The other night at the whisky bar Billy told me about a falling-out he had with Lewie Downer.

"Ferrr yirrrs Malcolm McSwain, Eddie Farmer, Lewie Downer and I played on Fridays. A menth agooo en e Freydayy, es usual Lewie wes hetting outt ef ternn. On thiii ninth grannnn I wes ewayyy end Lewie sterteddd pattting. Thirrr wes e secondd pettt end thinnn e therddd. Lewie thinn welked off thi grannnn taa thi tinth teee while wee finished outttt. Es wi welked to thi tee Lewie teed eff. I tirned te Malcolm end seid, 'Ef yurrr pertnerr dusn'tt steppp hetting uttt ef ternnn sumthingg es goingg tu heppen. I cen't teke et anymore.' Ettt continued fir thi runddd. Whinn wi wir dunnn end sittingg en thi clebhussse I tuld Malcommm niverr egeinn wuld I playyy weth Lewie."

A few weeks later in the locker Billy received an apology from Lewie at which time Billy interrupted and said, "Stuppp retttt thirrr. Aye dun't wenttt thess te gooo enyy fertherrr. We'errr dun."

Obviously, after thirty years Billy could take no more. Having heard that story I wasn't about to put myself in a situation where Billy would tell me to "stupppp rettt thirrr." I walk a little slower so Billy can keep up. Also, I make sure where everyone's ball is before I consider playing my shot. Actually, I am surprised to see him out in that cold wind after his recent stroke. I have a beanie pulled down over my golf hat, a wool sweater, and waterproofs over that. My head feels like it has been through a washing machine, as the wind blows. Billy only has a sweater on. I'm sure he can handle the cold better than I can.

The threesome has slowed up my play. The squall now is coming in for a direct hit. My intention is to wait it out at the rain shelter behind the 12th. Unfortunately, these boys are headed for the barn. I could have said my "goodbyes" and waited. Instead, I continue with them. The shower gets us on thirteen. They shelter under their umbrellas. I stand there without an umbrella. It only lasts for the hole, but we are pretty wet.

"Billy, are you starting to get your strength back?" I ask as Billy kneels down to catch his breath.

"Ettt simmms te cume en gooo. Ectuallly et 68 aye fillll es goot es aye ded et 28, which tills yuuuu aye wess weak thennn tooo," he says. "I can rimimber en Stableford whin I wuuuld gittt fortyyy points end todayyy I onlyyy gottt eyhteen." We both laugh. His stroke has gotten the best of him. Before the stroke he was strong as an ox. With jet-black hair combed straight back he commanded authority. That is what you need in a Caddy Master, so the caddies don't take advantage of the situation. With a subtle sense of humor and hardly a smile, he has some good stories.

"My mother said getting old was not for sissies," I come back.

"Ayeee," he says as he turns and looks at me with both a grin and a look in his eyes like he knows firsthand what my mom meant.

On the 18th as I line up my twenty foot putt Billy decides to give me advice on the line. "Jimmmm," he says, "this putt normally breaks a cup, bui always look et thi tide before yuuu putt. If it es going out et will break morrre. Loook!!! Thi tide is going outt. Play et to break two cups." My first thought is he must be kidding. However, he's the Caddy Master and I follow his advice. Sure enough, with the putt hit two cups out, the ball finds the bottom of the cup. I'll be paying attention to the direction of the tide in the future when I'm on the 18th green.

In the clubhouse our conversation continues. "I remember pleying e metch whirrr Eddie end I hed e best ball egainst Malcolm end Lewie. Wi wirr win ep going ento te thi tinth holl. Malcolm wes tin feet frim thi pin en twooo end I wes pin high lift of thi green en threee. Whin wi got te thi green Lewie picked ep my ball end hended et te meee. Malcolm missed thi birdie putt. Efter holing out he thin seid thi mitch wes eeevin. I rispinded, 'No, I git e fuuur also. Yurrr pertner picked ep my ball.' Malcolm looked rather flumaxed es hi gave Lewie thi eyeee.

"It only got bitter firrr holes latirrr whin I hittt e thinnn chip shot. Es it was getting close to going off the green I yelled 'stop,' at which time Lewie puuut hisss foot out end stopped thi ball. Lewie thin bint ovir te pick ep thi ball end I said 'leave et there.' Whin et wes my turnn te puuut es I started te address thi ball Malcolm said 'Yurrr out of thi hole. Yuuu hed him stop thi ball,' to which I said 'No I'm not. I wis tilling my ball te stoppp. I didn't telll yurrr partner te stick out hisss futtt te stop et.'

"With Malcolm ridddy te ixplode, I petted out fir e halve. Es weee played en Malcolm din't say enother worddd te Lewie Downer. Thi tinsion wes e bittt highhh. Eddie end I won thi match end probably e little more."

It was time for me to go, although I didn't want the stories to end. Saying my goodbyes I make a quick exit. "Tilll Lydia I wis esking fir hirr," he exclaims. Driving home I laughed out loud thinking about his stories.

26 BREAD DELIVERY

When I open the door of the house, I can smell the aroma of freshly-baked bread coming from the kitchen. Lydia decided a few weeks ago to make bread for the locals on a regular basis. What could be more welcoming than being given homemade bread?

With the bread wrapped in wax paper in a shopping bag, I head out to make deliveries. I decide the first delivery would be to Roddy McMichin who we bought our car from. Roddy is out, but his secretary Annie says he'll be back. The smell of the bread must have affected Annie. She starts telling me her life story before I can escape. "I'mmm en e neww relationship," she says. "He hes e furteen yirrr oldd end e sixteen yirr oldd. I'mm net surrr ebout thet, butt we're headed to Malta en e cuple offf weeks withuut thim. He seems veryyy nice."

I nod my head, as she goes on with her story. I wish I had an extra loaf of bread to give to her. "You are going to have the best time in Malta," I say as I leave I am glad I don't have to deal with new intimate relationships. Trying to change my golf swing is just about enough to deal with. I like the continuity of being married forty years to a lovely lass who, as a bonus, makes bread.

The next loaf of bread is going to Mari, the owner of La Vie en Rose Hair Salon. Mari is happy to see me. "Jimmmm, how er yuuuu," she asks.

"Fine," I reply. "Lydia has baked you bread."

"Thet ess soo niccce," as she gives me a kiss on the cheek. Before I can get out the door her mother comes out from the back. "Jimmmmm et is yuuuuu," she shouts. All of the sudden, I wish it wasn't me. Every patron in the beauty parlor is now looking at me. I can only give them a wide grin back. "Mariiiii seid lesttt timmm yuuuu wirrr herrre she esked yuuuu howww yuuuu likkedd thi cuttt end yuuuu seiddd cannn wiiii make et longgger. I wudddd heve seid F off." I continue to smile as I turn to the side, so I can prepare for what's coming. I figure she can't get as good a grip in the bear hug she is going to embrace me with. This woman is really strong. Delivering bread might not be a good idea after all. The deliveryman could get injured.

For the third loaf I walk around the corner of our house to the Ardshiel Hotel where Billy holds court in the whisky bar from 5:00

to 6:00 P.M. "Jimmmm, settt downnnn," he says as I slide sideways between people to get to Billy. I am still laughing thinking about the stories he had told at the clubhouse.

"Billy, Lydia has baked you a loaf of bread."

"Jimmmmm, till Lydia thank you very much," he says in an English accent despite being a native Campbeltonian. Then he adds, "She has soft hands." I can imagine how much Billy, three times engaged, but always a bachelor, enjoys fresh-baked bread.

Billy starts talking about his childhood. "My fither futtt en thi Warrr. He called me 'boyyy.' Daddd wes viry organized, fir exemple thi condiments wirrr erranged jist soo on thi table. He wes e fisherman with grendpaa. Et two A.M., all yirrr rundd they wouddd go to thi quay end diggg cockles uttt of thi muddd. Two hours latir they wulddd crack thi cockles end puttt thim en e thousand hooks. They thin boateddd into thi bay where thi lines wirr drupped. Efter a few hours of sleep et thi house, they wuldd return end bring in thi lines teaming with cod, haddock and uther white fish. Et wis a harddd life."

"It sounds very hard," I reply.

With a lager in hand Billy continues. "Jimmmm, yuuu prubably doin't know, bettt I wis e butcher bifore I wis thi Caddyyy Masterrr. Myyy fist dayyy en thi job I plucked chickens. Whinn I

154

gottt hommme my muther noticed sumething en my shuuulder. I was covered in liiice. 'You're nit going beck te thit butcher shoppp' she screamed. I worked as a butcher thi nixt thirty years."

As I say goodbye, Billy says, "Tell Lydia I wis esking about her." Walking out of the hotel, I can see Billy in the window of the bar. He is sitting with his back to the front window. It is a nice place to spend an evening. Flora, the owner, is behind the bar waiting on customers. The people are jammed in the small space. It is a lively scene. However, I am opting out for the quiet of the cottage. Lydia and I will sit in the living room reading while the sun goes down. With any luck it will be a beautiful sunset.

27 THE LILY POND

Tomorrow I'm headed to Kilberry to help John Caskey clean out
his lily pond. As a precaution for that drive, I go into Side Motors
to have Willy check the ignition on the Vauxhall Meriva. It seems
that the starting is a bit random lately, not starting up every time.
Willy tries it. "Thet es thi bist e diesell well doo," he says. "I'mmm
goinggg te put in en additivvv te cleeen outtt thi enjicccters."

With that done I ask, "End whet do I owe yuuu?"

"Thi compuuterrr esn't onnn, so geve me e wee shout simmm
timme." Nodding I remember this is the same guy who diagnosed
my immobilization fault in the car computer as a "wee gremlin." I
think he was right about the gremlin because it seems to have left
and the car starts fine. I'll give him a "wee shout" later in the week.
He tells me not to fill up the tank, so the additive will work
properly.

The next morning at 7:30 A.M., I head out for Kilberry. Arriving at five to nine, John tells me I am early. I am indeed, by five minutes on a one and a half hour drive. With the hip boots I've borrowed from Johnny at Alladin's Cave and yellow rubber gloves I'd found at the newsagent in hand, I head to the pond.

John is quite a sight. He has Kleenex up one nostril covered in blood. He must have some bleeding issues. He insists on putting his hip boots on over my objection. I don't want to have to pull an old man out of the pond. It will be hard enough getting the weeds out without also pulling out a body.

Using a rake and fork like walking poles I walk into the pond. It is three feet deep where the bog weed has collected. I start pulling it out with the rake. It works pretty well but seems to pull up the grassy bottom of the pool. The rake makes it hard physical work, as it grabs the bottom. It looks like it will take three hours to get the weed out. I won't last that long using the rake. I think of what a Chinese coolie would do in a rice paddy and go at a more leisurely pace using my hands to pull out the weed. The rhizomes of the bog weed are an inch thick and trail forever. What I should have brought was my midgie net because with each disturbance of the weeds, midgies swarm my head giving a warm sensation on my forehead as they bite.

I am distracted by the bench on the side of the pond remembering visits from before when Kathleen would tell me to sit beside her.

Without Kathleen sitting there, the bench looks cold and hard. If the bench has a mind, it must wonder where Kathleen is. I then think of her first words to me whenever I would see her. She would do most of the talking, as Lydia and John stood. It felt awkward sitting with her, but I always obey the command of a pipe-smoking artist suffering from Asperger's Syndrome. The disease seemed to kick in on my arrival at her door. "I am looking for the artist Kathleen Russell," I would say with her standing in the doorway. "Yuuuu fuuuuuuckking, dick, fuuuuckking, shittt," she would mutter. A delightful lady in a carefree bohemian sort of way, it is nice to remember her on the bench as I'm getting the weeds out of the pond.

John is working in an area of the pond. He stops every now and then to catch his breath. He has a heart condition. The tissue up his nose is totally soaked in blood. It is not the best sight. I try not to look his direction. I decide that if he collapses in the pond, it won't be that difficult to get him out. He doesn't weigh that much and the pond isn't very deep. "Jimmmm, whirrr yirrr forkkk es stopp thirrr," he says as he points to the pitchfork in the pond. He has a good eye for beauty when it comes to plants and I'm sure he thought the pond would look better with some vegetation in that area. My deforestation in the pond started at the lilies and worked back to the side of the pond. The bog weed beyond the fork is saved.

"John," I say. "The willows need to be cut back."

"Littt's nett worrry abuttt ett now," he replies.

"John, get me some loping cutters and a saw." With the tools in hand I cut the willows back to the bigger wood. Where they had been lying in the pond, they are now gracefully hanging over the pond. I am surprised at how much wood I have cut.

"Livvvve et thirrr," he says.

Finding out where his burn pile is, I pull the dead branches out of the pond to the back of his property. "John, let's cut back the Gunner plant, so people don't run into the bench which is hidden." The large Gunner plant has leaves draping and concealing one of the many wooden benches in the garden. With those leaves cut we are done.

"Wuuuud yuuuu likkk teaaa er coffeeee?"

"No, thank you," I reply. "I'll just have a glass of water." As I sit in the kitchen, I look at the menagerie of things that are there including a stuffed otter, a glass case with twelve stuffed birds, a rope and pulley system with slats to hang drying clothes when hoisted to the ceiling, a wooden screen from the far east, and a wood floor, ceiling and cabinets painted by his deceased wife. If you then consider the additional one hundred items randomly situated along with cooking pots and pans stacked on the stove, it is a bit of a clutter. It makes it hard to walk through and more difficult to sit down.

I had told John I was low on diesel. I planned on filling up in Tarbert only to find they don't have a petrol station. Before I arrived at Kilberry, the red indicator light for the fuel came on. I didn't think I could make it back without a few liters of diesel. John assured me he could syphon some diesel out of his vehicle to a petrol can.

After a few minutes of talking about cricket, which I know nothing about, we go outside for the siphoning project. John rummages through his shed. With an old gasoline can and a hose, John is ready for the job. With the hose in the tank John tries to create enough suction. He acts like he knows what he is doing. I think he might pass out as he inhales.

"I'm sorry I don't think I can help," he says after getting his breath back. I then realize that he doesn't know anything about siphoning, because he quit much too quickly. I consider trying it. I quickly change my mind. There is no way I am going to suck on that hose knowing diesel will be on its way into my mouth. John then wants to see where my petrol gauge is. "Yer on the blinking light," he informs me. This is not news to me.

"Gooood luckkk," he says as I start the engine. Still trying to find diesel I go next door to the Kilberry Inn, but Richard has gone to town. As I come out of the building, I see the wood-burning artist

Kennedy cleaning his wheelie bin across the street. I think this might be a stroke of luck, until I get his answer, "I'vvv nooo dieselll."

As I think about what just happened, I realize John is too old to figure out how he can help me. He should be following me in his car as I drive to Tarbert. It is not every day some American cleans out your lily pond. Actually, I really did this for Kathleen. I still owed her for a painting we traded out. When she received the pomegranate bush in the mail it was much smaller than advertised. Then it died a short time later, even with the agronomist from King's College, John, nurturing it. I always felt as though she hadn't gotten a fair deal on the painting. With the lily pond cleaned out, I feel much better about seeing the abstract painting at the top of our stairs.

I now have a choice. It is twenty miles to Lochgilphead and fourteen miles to Tarbert. Figuring it was more of a climb to Lochgilphead, I head to Tarbert. As I leave Kilberry, Richard in his black Audi TT is coming at me at a high rate of speed on the single-track road. Without a turn out and me in my coasting mode I keep going, pulling into the burrow pit as I pass Richard. He probably thinks I am nuts driving through the grass ditch but I can explain it to him on Monday when we play golf.

It is more uphill than I thought. I coast half the way, but the fourteen miles seem to go on forever. It is curious how my body sways forward in the car, as I'm going uphill trying to get more out of the glide. The moving back and forth of my body must look quite strange to a passerby.

Coasting the last two miles I glide into the Tarbert golf course. The superintendent only has red diesel. Starting the car up I hold my breath the final mile to Tarbert hill, where I coast into the village and pull into a tight parking place with the car off and no power steering. The problem with running out of diesel is that the lines have to be bled before the car will start again.

I go into David Fletcher's for a sandwich. "David, my car's empty. Do you know where I can get diesel?" I ask.

"Aye dontt likke diesel," is his reply. Really? I wasn't asking preferences. Someone in the shop says perhaps the boatmen at the dock could help. David quickly says, "They use red diesel."

"So David, if I hitchhike to Clachan, is there somewhere in Tarbert I can get a petrol can?" I ask.

"Nooooo, yellll need te gitt thet en Clachan," he says with his eyes bulging out of his gaunt face, which is looking around and twitching as he speaks. I was hoping that question would get some sympathy if not help.

In walks a lady, and without missing a beat David with his face still moving about says, "I wess jestt thinking aboutt yuuuu." I can only imagine what he was thinking about. I heard the same line out of David the previous week. He has quickly moved on from my problem to thinking about girls.

I walk next door to Stuart Herd's gallery. Luckily, Stuart was there and not the talkative female salesman who says too much in her description of the painting of Colonsay that is still for sale. "Stuart, I'm out of diesel. Is there anywhere in town I can get a couple of liters?" I ask. "Aye, jest go bihiiind me to thi graggg." Now I'm getting somewhere.

Winding up the hill, which seemed more than just behind his shop, I can see in the distance Hi Lo Motors. Telling the mechanic my problem, he says there is a diesel tank outside the building, but it isn't his. Possibly the owner, Duncan, would be in the Post Office. I tell Stuart what the mechanic has said, and he points across the street to the Post Office.

"Is Duncan in?" I ask. "Aye," comes the reply. Explaining my problem, Duncan is more than happy to sell me a full tank of diesel. What a relief to have diesel in the car. I realize at this moment that I am no longer holding my breath.

On my way back to Campbeltown, I stop at the Glenbarr Village Store for advice from Peter. Seeing him in the nursery I say, "Peter. I'm surprised you're still here." He laughs at the comment, since he spends sixteen hours a day there. "Can you tell me how to take care of the dahlias and begonias when winter sets in." He explains in detail they are tubers, which need to be dried out in the winter and planted again in May.

Back in Campbeltown, Lydia has made homemade bread to give to Johnny who lent me the hip boots. With boots in one hand and hot French bread in the other I walk over to his shop. "Johnny, I can't thank you enough."

"My pleasssure," he replies. Johnny has the "gift of gab." After a day in the lily pond and a harrowing drive, I just want to get home. As soon as he takes a breath in his conversation, I say goodbye and make a quick exit. I need to sit down.

28 THE PROPRIETOR OF
THE KILBERRY INN

When we had dinner at the Kilberry Inn a few weeks ago, the proprietor, Richard Stilton and I arranged a game on a Monday in a fortnight. Most of his golf is played in the winter, which is the off-season for an innkeeper. After bringing our drinks to the table, he stood back and said, "Whet doo yuu think?" as he took a practice swing without a club. Before I could answer he continued, "Et es right hirrr." He kept his right wrist in a wedge going back and his right elbow at the top of the swing a few inches from his side. I nodded my head as he crouched over and repeated the move while maintaining eye contact. With a grin on his face, he continued, "Aye think I'vvve get et. Aye hivvv e nettt behind thi restaurant. I'mm hitting billls iverydayyy."

"Let's play when you can get away," I said.

"Pleassurrre," Richard said, and the game was set.

When he came back with the food, monkfish for me and salmon for Lydia, he said, "In thi Fall I'm going te Askernish Golf Club en thi Outer Hebrides. Et's en Oldd Tomm Morris coursss thet hes binn brought beck te life. I'll givvv yuuu e riport efter I've played et." I haven't been to the Outer Hebrides yet, but I know that Scarista on South Harris is a favorite of Nick Faldo. I hope I get there.

"Es thirrr enything else I cen git yuuu?" he asked.

"I think we're good," I replied.

"Goodo," he said as he headed into the kitchen.

This Michelin-rated restaurant in the village of Kilberry, population eighty-five, is a real treat. Situated on a single-track road, forty miles from Machrihanish, it is in a remote place. The views of Jura and Islay in the distance are breathtaking, as you look out on the Irish Sea. Arriving at the Inn you are always greeted by Richard behind the bar. "Whet wuldd yuuu likkk to drenk?" he asks. The place has a familiar feel. A fire is burning in the fireplace. It is worth the drive just to have the chocolate crème brûlèe, a scoop of mascarpone sorbet and a biscuit.

The Monday golf game with Richard arrives. I had invited David

Edwards, an embryologist from Gullane to join us. David stays in a caravan when he comes to Machrihanish. I like that. His house in Gullane, which he pronounces "Gillin," is a sandstone Victorian. When he comes to play golf, he is perfectly happy with a 6' X 12' trailer. I'm amazed it doesn't blow away in a gale. He plays with a mismatched set of clubs slung over his shoulder in a small carry bag. The putter is a trusty old Callaway Tuttle mallet head. His swing is long and flowing. He's obviously played a lot of golf.

David and I meet Richard on the first tee. He has brought a friend, Ian, to fill out the foursome. With brief introductions it is agreed that David and I will take them on in a best ball. After figuring out the handicaps, the match is on. Ian is excited to hit his drive over the beach. A little too excited, he ends up on the beach. David and I are giving up a lot of shots in this match, so we will have to play well. I knew this round would be a nice change for Richard. He is too busy at the Inn in the summer to get in much golf. Nevertheless, he practices a lot. When not hitting into the net behind the Inn, he goes down to the beach and hits balls. Hector has told him he needs to hit the ball first and then take a divot. The beach is good practice for that. An actual round of golf at Machrihanish will be a nice change for him.

I had forgotten, since I last played with Richard, about both the energy and the unusual mannerisms he has on the golf course. Before he hits his tee shot, he faces the sea with a tee in the ground and takes a powerful practice swing. Turning toward the fairway and addressing the ball he gives it an equally hard swing. Grunting as he makes contact his ball slices into the 18th fairway. It is easy to bail out on the first hole at Machrihanish, especially after your partner has hit his ball on the beach.

On the green Richard is equally animated and serious. When it is his turn to putt, he quickly gets to the ball. "Take it away," he says, referring to the flag, which I am tending. After crouching over to see the line, he gives a tomahawk motion with his right arm and then stands to address the ball. All of his actions are quick and lively. However, his putting stroke is tentative. The ball "peedles" short of the hole, as though, it has no intention of ever going in.

As we stand on the 8th tee we can see a sliver of the fairway in the distance. A massive sand dune on the left blocks the flight of any balls trying to carry it. The green is visible looking like a tabletop perched on another sand dune. To hit the green on the second shot the player needs to be hitting a seven iron or less. Even at that, the second shot will look good in the air, but come up short because you can't feel the wind that is blowing on top. The short shot rolls forty yards back to the bottom of the dune.

We all hit good drives. To my surprise the second shots are equally good. I've never seen four balls on this green before. Richard knocks in his birdie putt to win the hole.

The match is close. I can see that Richard wants to focus on the game, so it is no time for small talk. Enjoying watching his continuous motion, I pay closer attention. Before hitting the ball, Richard's face twitches and his shoulders move forward and backward. He continues to make a grunting sound like Maria Sharapova when he hits his driver. On the green he is always moving, swinging his right arm over his head and moving his feet like he is dancing. He gives the feeling of a boxer getting ready for the next round.

With the match dormie, two up with two to go, I snap one out of bounds on 17. The tee points right where the O.B. is. I don't hit many shots left anymore. It was just a poor shot; a double-cross at the wrong time. I say to Richard, "I've given you an opening."

"Seize the day," he responds and pushes his ball into the second fairway. Actually, that is a good place to play from. On the green, however, David knocks in a putt with that old Callaway mallet putter.

"Well done, David," I say as I shake his hand. David has a smile on his face after sending his ball into the hole. Thanking our competitors, we go ahead and play the last hole.

As we sit in the clubhouse, we talk about the proposed wind farm the government is planning to put in the pristine water of the bay. Apparently, the Royals own the sea shelf and will be leasing it to the wind farm company. The government report had said it would be a perfect place for wind turbines, due to the shallow shelf in the water and the fact that there were no views. They must be sightless because the views might be the best in the world. On a clear day like this, the Irish Sea was almost calm at low tide. The islands in the distance seem close enough to touch. The humps of Jura are majestic. Twelve miles to the south, Northern Ireland is equally appealing. This is not a room with a view but an entire coastline with a view. Hopefully the public outcry will stop the wind farm development. It wouldn't be the same walking down the first fairway of Machrihanish with rows of tall white turbines in the sea.

Richard says, "Whin yuuu come upp nixt time, cell ahead, end I'llll puttt monkfish on thi menu end crème brûlèe."

"Sunday it is," I respond.

"Goodo, I'll see you then," he says. With the drinks finished, we head our separate ways. Richard is headed back to Kilberry with his guest.

David is headed to his caravan in the holiday park, about four hundred yards away, overlooking the ladies' course. "Jimmm," he says. "I heve e CD fir yuuu, 'Local Hero.' I think yuuu'll like it."

29 WHAT HAPPENED TO THE GREENS?

In March I received some bad news from Machrihanish's pro, Hector McDonald. "Jimmm thiiii greenns ere verrry beddd. Thirrr es morrr dirttt showing thennn gressss." The previous year the greens had not been sprayed, aerated and verticutt on a regular basis. With winter rains and compacted greens, much of the grass died out. At the thirteenth hour, the green keeper decided to deep core the greens. Starting at the practice green, he operated the core machine to the horror of the Machrihanish Committee members present. He moved the machine too fast, as the tines went into the ground. Instead of coring, it ripped up sections of the green.

"Whet es hi doing too ere green," yelled out thi Captain. "We'll nutt be duinng thet." The Committee told him to stop right there.

A golf course is really not a golf course without well-manicured tees and greens. If they are not in good condition it is just a piece of land where you practice hitting shots—nothing more than a glorified driving range. The mystery of golf is in getting the ball into the hole. To accomplish that it begins at the tee. Since the driver is for most people the most difficult club to hit in the bag, the tee needs to be in perfect condition. It needs to be level with closely mowed grass. An uneven tee is a mental block for the golfer. With the ball on the tee, instead of concentrating on hitting the ball, he thinks more about his feet in a low spot on the tee while addressing the ball, which is teed up on a thin patch of grass that is sloped. It probably shouldn't bother the player that much, but it does.

Then once the ball finds the green how can you get it in the hole if it doesn't roll well? As you stand over the putt looking at the different heights of grasses between the ball and the pin, you think, "What is the use?" It is then confirmed as the ball bounces along in an erratic manner and stops three feet short. The three-footer that remains is no game. Trying to ram it into the cup, so that it stays on line, it goes off like a shettleston harrier at full gait. It catches part of the cup, but doesn't go in. It's another bogey. Even though you were on the green in regulation, there was no chance at a birdie. Having a great short game from off the green isn't going to help either. It is unlikely in these conditions to get up and down from one hundred yards out.

I've learned a Maine expression while working on a course there. Golfers in Maine say a golf course is "tees and greens." If those two areas are in good shape, the condition of the fairways can be dealt with. Greens need to have enough speed to roll the ball. Likewise, they need to be smooth enough to keep the ball on line. Without a good surface you could hit eighteen greens in regulation and shoot ninety with a three putt on every hole. That is not golf.

Even with a good putting surface, the superintendent has to be ever vigilant in their care. Although greens might look good on the surface, it is what is underneath which determines whether the greens will be playable a month from now.

"Loook et thi butifulll coloooor of thi greens," the Captain explains to a Committee member.

"Aye," comes the reply, "a butifulll sittte et esss. Aren't wi luckkky?"

Little do they know of what lurks underneath? The color on the surface of the green doesn't tell the story of its condition. By April Machrihanish had eighteen temporary greens. News travels fast between golfers when a course has bad greens. The pro shop got one call after another from tour groups inquiring about their condition and then canceling their tee times.

When I arrive in June I am hoping for the best. I'm excited to be back at Machrihanish. Although I've been practicing Stack and Tilt over the winter, it has not progressed as fast as I would like without having Hector McDonald watching. As I walk up the small path to the pro shop, the practice green looks as though it is ground under repair. The grass is thin. It has brown dirt patches throughout.

Walking into the pro shop I am greeted by Craig, the assistant pro. "Jimmmm wilcomm back."

Fiona walks up from the other end of the shop and gives me a hug, "Jimmm ets goot te seee yuuu."

The pro's door opens and with a smile on his face, McDonald says, "Myyy favarittt pupil." It is good to be back. Hector continues by saying, "Thii greens aren'tt goot butt they ere puttablle. Thivvv started to fill en weth thi warmer timperture. Thirr aren'tt any temporaries."

"I can make do. Can we set up a lesson?" I ask.

"Tomorrow at 10:00," Hector replies.

With the lesson set up I head out to play. The ocean smell is just the same. The turf has that same bounce under foot. The oystercatchers are quickly moving on the beach feeding as the surf goes out. And oh yes, the greens; they are in poor condition. The ball acts like a drunken sailor as it wobbles toward the hole. At a speed of perhaps 6 on the Stimpmeter, they are a sharp contrast to the perfect bent greens I have been playing in Las Vegas.

Going into the clubhouse I notice an agronomy report is posted on the board. It outlines a detailed program to get the greens and tees in good shape by removing the thatch and organic material. A program of aerating, verticutting and sanding the tees and greens would get the greens back to where they need to be. As I play over the next two months I keep watching for the maintenance program to begin. It never does. A thick layer of thatch is still blocking the roots. The surface now has Fairy Ring fungus making unusual circular designs. With the fall approaching and the growing season getting shorter the greenskeeper is running out of time. I wonder why the agronomist's program hasn't been followed.

Ultimately, I decide to send a letter to the Captain and Committee voicing my concerns. As an American member of the club I am not sure how it will be received, but I don't care. I am more concerned about the greens. If the Captain doesn't like my input, I will be fine with that. The letter reads as follows:

Dear Sirs:

It is great to be back at Machrihanish. The last four weeks have gone by too fast. I have enjoyed the golf. The greens are rolling well. I am glad the course has come along since February. Nevertheless, looks are sometimes deceiving especially with greens. The important item is what is underneath.

Unfortunately, Machrihanish greens have a layer of thatch and organic material which blocks the roots.

The last ten years I have worked at different times on a Donald Ross course in Maine called Lucerne Golf Club. When I am there, I mow greens and fairways along with verticutting, tining greens and tee boxes. This last year in Maine it rained all winter. When we arrived in May to open the course at Lucerne, the greens were in perfect condition. Other courses in the area, including Arrostock Golf Club, lost their greens. The only reason Lucerne had greens, and the others didn't, was vigorous greens maintenance, which gets rid of thatch and provides drainage along with a spraying program for fungus. On arrival in May the first thing we did was begin the program again.

In the four weeks I've been here I've seen evidence of one light verticuting. That is not enough to remove the thatch. Summer is speeding by. So is the time within which vigorous verticutting and tining can be done on the greens to promote strong root growth. Additionally tee boxes need coring and sanding for proper drainage to promote grass growth. If a program is established, the greens will always make it through the winter.

This is a wonderful golf course. In Maine golf course are all about "tees and greens." If they're in good condition, golfers are happy. The same should be true here.

Sincerely yours,
Jim Wedge

The reply from the Captain was slow in coming. It consisted of a very proper thank you for my interest in the course condition. It went on to say I could be well assured the Committee was following the maintenance program. I later learned the Captain's exact words were more like "thet Emericann cen take hes arse end shuvv et." The Captain's actual words of rebuke were consistent with what happened on the golf course the next two months in the way of following a maintenance program: little or nothing. He obviously knows little about conditioning a golf course. You'd think he would have relied on the report and then acted on it. I can only imagine how much more frustrating this situation must be to Hector McDonald, the golf professional. He must just shake his head in dismay as he looks out over the first tee and practice green. No one seems to be asking him what needs to be done to get the course in good shape. If they are asking, they aren't following his suggestions.

30 THE NEXT DAY'S LESSON

Waking the next morning and looking out the bedroom window to the garden, I have to pinch myself to make sure I am not dreaming. As I turn over and look out the window, the garden view looks distorted. I then realize I am in Scotland. The 1820's glass panes in the window have swirls in them. They are beautiful.

I'm looking forward to my golf lesson this morning. My last lesson was nine months ago. Since then, I've been playing golf regularly in Las Vegas at a place called Spanish Trail. The changes that Hector McDonald has made in my swing have lowered my scores. My brother no longer gives me shots. Instead, we are playing even. My handicap is now a six. I think my brother was in disbelief that my game had improved, given that my game had been the same for the last thirty years. I remember each spring it felt like a New Year for my golf game. I was sure I would play better, as I eagerly looked forward to the Masters in April. However, by August the dog days of summer arrived and my golf game was still the same.

My golf swing was very vertical. On the takeaway the club went outside and looped as it came down steeply. I was always fighting the club being closed at impact. Hitting few greens in regulation I had to rely on my short game to score. That isn't the case anymore. Instead, the club stays on plane as I go from flexion in my hips to extension of the back on the backswing. It looks flat, but it isn't. It's on plane. Without any adjustment on the downswing I'm able to hit down on the ball with a shallow divot beginning at the ball. I come out of the ground on the follow-through with my back extending again.

When I got to Vegas nine months ago, I wanted to keep improving. Once a month, I recorded a video of my swing from the side and from the back, using an iPhone attached to a small tripod. Hector McDonald would pull up the videos on the computer using a program called Dropbox. When he put them back in Dropbox the videos had lines overlaying my swing and voice over with instruction.

The first video went like this: "OK Jimmm en thes wonn aye wuldd likkk te seee thi balll moved winn balll back frum thi left fuut—yurr hends en front of thi balll. Yuuu see whet heppens hirrr. Yurr olde nemesis thi hends move forward es yuuu go back. Et's e bigg improvement bett wi wulddd rither seee yurrr hends settt up like thet. Yuuu'll stay on thi plane much better weth thi clebface more open. You'll be able te hit thi balll more up en thi airrr. All thi other things ere going to be sooo much betterrr."

His teaching from the video was a big help through the winter. Each month he pointed out problems I was dealing with in the swing. What we think the swing is doing is quite different from what a video reveals. Hector's commentary pointed out continuing problems I needed to work on.

Looking at the backswing from behind he'd say, "OK, herrr wi go en thi backswing. Yurrr hands shulddd be moving en more. Et thi top of thi swinggg yurrr left arm es matching thi shoulder, ok. Thi clubface es closed a bittt, because thi swing es abovve thi bluuu line. Et impact thi right armmm es not in enuff. It shulddd have been en twenty degrees to thi baseline. Es e result yurrr hands heve rollled over. Et thi finish yurrr spine angle es now….. ah, 60 degrees—thet es really goot—et should be 50 degrees."

In the first lesson a year ago Hector said this change of the swing would be a slow process, "bettt sooo worth et."

"Jimmm, yuuu won't git ell these angles and positions correct. Wi wentt to git yuuu es close es wi can. Coming uttt of flexion to extension thi ideal wulddd be herrr," as he leaned towards the target, "but yuuu probably won't gitt thirrr—but we'll git yuuu close. Et will be sooo much betterrr. Rimember to cummm outtt of thi grounddd et impact." It is important to remember that the improvement may never get to the perfect swing. The important point is that the improvements are going in that direction. Likewise, it requires a great deal of patience as the changes are made and balls miss-hit.

"Softly, softly, catchee monkey," Hector calls the incremental changes in the swing.

As I drive out to Machrihanish, I think of where my swing is now. At address, I bend over more with my feet pointed out. The left hand grips the club in a strong position with the right hand in a neutral position with a short right thumb. There is no trigger finger. I grip the club firmly. The left shoulder, turning under, starts the club back and up. I still have a problem taking it back too low, which separates my hands from my body. As the club goes back, it should be even closer inside, but at least it is in a better position. Trying to keep the wedge in my wrists as well as the same distance between my forearms throughout the backswing, I have a much bigger shoulder turn while the club doesn't go back as far. With my right leg almost straight and the left leg bent the downward motion requires weight on the left foot and then a straightening of that leg in order to come out of the ground. I no longer chase after the ball.

Hector's advice for hitting a golf ball a long way boils down to a player taking advantage of three different motions. "Jimmmm, thi swinggg hes threee parttts: thi shoulders terning, thi axmannn and sliding towards thi target. Looook et my extinsion whin I doooo thissss," Hector has repeated to me. He would show me the axman by raising his hands over his head while standing very tall and looking like Paul Bunyan. He then would bend from the waist to the left and turn his shoulders. "Looook et how strong these es," he would continue. And then, as if choreographed, he would go directly to the next motion sliding the legs through impact. "Jimmm, yurrrrr lift knee slides forward end et impact yurrrr belt es en frunt of yuuur foottt. Looook, yuuuu ere cintered wherrr thi belll wes et thi addrisss," he would say. By using the three motions, "thii swinggg es soooo mich betterrr".

Arriving at Machrihanish, McDonald has his video equipment, practice balls and training aids in the buggie. "Jimmm, let's see wherrr yurrr et with yurrr swinggg. Hittt sommm seven irons forr me." With that the lesson begins. The seven irons are hit crisply with a shallow divot at the ball, and my body rises up in the finish. The sand dunes in the background make it easy to follow the flight of the balls. The balls look like they have a purpose as they make the same flight through the air—they start just to the right with a slight hook. Hector McDonald finally speaks, "Jimmm, thi improvement es goot. We're going te make et even betterrr."

Bobby Blair and Ronald McFair arrive for a game tomorrow. It will be nice to see improvement in Bobby's swing. Nothing would make him happier. Golfers are all the same. We always have this hope in the back of our minds that some change in our swing will make us a better player. Luckily, I've replaced that hope with a method of instruction, which is in fact bringing my handicap down. Golf is so much more fun when it is played well. That said, the process for improving one's game can be enjoyable in itself, especially at a magical place like Machrihanish Golf Club.

THE END

ABOUT THE AUTHOR

After twenty-six years of criminal defense, J.L. discovered a unique golf course in a remote part of Scotland. He now spends his summers there. Like all golfers wanting to improve their game, he started taking golf lessons three years ago. The lessons have required a complete swing change which led to the story for this book. He is still taking lessons.

Made in the USA
San Bernardino, CA
12 January 2015